MW00837717

"Generative AI is poised to shape, even disrupt, many sectors of society. And as such, everyone is well-advised to think carefully about how it will impact their jobs and organizations. This book provides the perfect perspective for CEOs and leaders of other organizations, written by a leader who is at the vanguard of understanding and shaping this new, powerful technology. Full of crystal-clear explanations, anecdotes from the author's own experiences, and actionable recommendations, this book is essential for any leader interested in keeping up with the times."

—**Prof. Peter Stone, professor of computer science at UT Austin, director of Texas Robotics, and executive director of Sony AI America**

"Amir Husain's *Generative AI for Leaders* is the indispensable companion for CEOs, C-suite executives, and managers trying to cut through the AI fog to understand what Generative AI can do for their companies. Amir dispenses with the hype and focuses on the nuts and bolts of what it takes to bring Generative AI capabilities to bear in any industry. This user-friendly playbook will get you started on the right path immediately, and help you find the strategic advantage you've been looking for. Don't wait for your competitors to beat you to the punch!"

—**Lieutenant General John (Jack) N.T. Shanahan (USAF, Ret.), inaugural director of the U.S. Department of Defense Joint AI Center**

"Understanding Generative AI is no longer just an option for CEOs and other C-level executives but has become a business imperative. Amir's latest book is a timely response to the challenges faced by leaders, around the world, who are seeking to successfully lead in an era of technological, political and business disruptions. It seamlessly blends strategic insights with real-world applications, offering a holistic understanding of how Generative AI can be integrated into existing operations to help executives create competitive strategic advantage, drive digital transformation, spur innovation, and shape the future of their organizations."

—**Vinod Philip, Executive Board Member and Chief Technology Officer at Siemens Energy**

PRAISE FOR *THE SENTIENT MACHINE* BY AMIR HUSAIN

"A must-read for anyone looking to understand how artificial intelligence is poised to transform human society and life. Husain is not only an engineer and entrepreneur, but also a philosopher who thinks deeply about what AI will mean for humanity."

—Paul Scharre, Author of *Four Battlegrounds: Power in the Age of Artificial Intelligence*

"By situating the conversation around opportunities for AI to improve or extend our lives, this book provides a rational argument and reassurance to general readers fearful of an increasingly AI-infused future."

—*Library Journal*

"Husain argues that the only way to deter intentional misuse [of A.I.] is to develop bellicose A.N.I. of our own: 'The 'choice' is really no choice at all: we must fight AI with AI.' If so, A.I. is already forcing us to develop stronger A.I."

—*The New Yorker*

"AI may be the most profound force shaping every dimension of human existence in the 21st century. In this landmark book, Amir Husain lays bare not only the science of AI, but the many sectors in which AI will find a prominent role. *The Sentient Machine* is a must-read for all those who will live with the realities of the 'AI Century.'"

—General John R. Allen, USMC (Ret.) Former Commander, NATO International Security Assistance Force and U.S. Forces Afghanistan

"Whether you are a business leader, policy maker, or entrepreneur, you need to understand Artificial Intelligence and its power to shape our future. In his brilliantly written book, Amir Husain, one of the world's leading AI experts, will help you gain that understanding."

—John Chambers, Chairman Emeritus, Cisco Systems and Founder and CEO, JC2 Ventures

Generative AI for Leaders

Amir Husain (@amirhusain_tx)

Title: Generative AI for Leaders / Amir Husain.
Description: First edition. | Austin, TX: AM Press, [2023] | Includes index.

ISBN: 979-8-9884751-2-5 (paperback)
ISBN: 979-8-9884751-0-1 (hardcover)

For my Father,
Who taught me how to learn

Contents

Chapter 1

Introduction

1.1 What is Generative AI?

Generative AI is a sub-field of artificial intelligence with the potential to shape the future. This branch of AI brings a creative aspect to machine intelligence, allowing it to not just analyze and interpret data but also to generate new content. This content can take various forms, from the written word to visual images, music, and even the development of digital environments.

To understand the essence of Generative AI, one must delve into the realm of machine learning, a branch of AI that focuses on enabling computers to learn from experience, somewhat akin to how humans learn. Traditional machine learning models learn from existing data to make predictions or decisions. They are "discriminative," classifying input data into defined categories. However, Generative AI goes a step further.

In a sea of data, generative models find not just patterns but the underlying distribution that governs the data. They utilize this knowledge to generate new instances of data that share the characteristics of the original dataset. Thus, a generative model trained on a dataset of paintings can produce new images that echo the artistic styles it has learned.

Two significant types of generative models have emerged as front runners in the field: Generative Adversarial Networks (GANs) and Transformer-based models. GANs are an ingenious construct, where two neural networks—the generator and the discriminator—are pitted against each other in a competitive game. The generator creates new data instances, and the discriminator evaluates them. Over time, through this adversarial process, the generator learns to create data that is almost indistinguishable from the real data.

On the other hand, Transformer-based models, like the immensely popular generative pre-training Transformer (GPT) releases, GPT-3 and GPT-4, use the concept of attention to generate text that is contextually relevant. They capture the dependencies between words and their contexts in the text, enabling the generation of coherent and contextually accurate sentences. While GANs have found wide application in image and music generation, Transformer-based models have revolutionized text generation.

The magic of Generative AI lies in its creative potential. It can compose music, create visual art, design products, and write convincing text. It can even develop video game levels or create simulations for virtual reality environments. Such capabilities were once thought to be exclusively human, but Generative AI is changing that idea.

However, like any technology, it is not without its complexities. Generative AI models require substantial computational resources and training data. They also demand a deep under-standing of machine learning principles to effectively guide their learning process. The generated content can also be subject to the biases inherent in the training data, which may result in unintended and potentially harmful consequences.

In essence, Generative AI is not just a technological innovation; it is a new canvas for creativity, a new tool for problem solving, and a new frontier for exploration. It promises to reshape our relationship with technology, blurring the lines between human and machine creativity, and opening up a world of possibilities that are as exciting as they are perplexing. As we stand on the precipice of this new era, it is up to us to harness its potential responsibly, navigating the challenges and embracing the opportunities that Generative AI brings to our doorstep.

As we venture further into this chapter and the ones that follow, we will unravel the layers of Generative AI, delving into its benefits and challenges, its applications, and its potential future. We will explore why it matters to leaders and how it can be harnessed to drive innovation, productivity, and growth.

1.2   Developing an Intuitive Understanding

Let's unpack how Generative AI works. Take, for instance, GPT-3. It operates by completing a phrase like "Mary had a little..." Most people would complete that phrase by saying "Mary had a little lamb" because that line is from a famous children's nursery rhyme. Essentially, because a person has heard it before, they possess a mental model that can predict the next word when given a partial sentence.

This principle underlies the workings of large language models, a type of Generative AI. Models like GPT-3 and GPT-4, predict the next word in a sequence. However, before making this prediction, these models compute Word Embeddings, which capture the relationships among words. They consider not just a few words, but dozens and even hundreds. This focus on relationships allows the models to extract the rules of grammar, semantics, and more, going beyond merely predicting the next word.

1.2.1   Is Everything a Sequence?

Consider that a word is simply a token or an element in a sequence. A sentence defines a sequence, and a word may be the next token in that sequence. This idea extends to pixels—the small dots of color that make up an image. Like words, pixels can also be predicted in a sequence, with the color and intensity of the pixel being items a user wants to predict or generate.

The concept of prediction doesn't stop at pixels and words. Humans can also predict actions. For instance, if we see a curvature in the arm of a baseball pitcher along with the ball in his hand, we can generally predict what will happen next. He's about to throw the ball.

What's intriguing is how much human activity consists of one action following another and how much human intelligence can be encapsulated by understanding the relationship of actions, tokens, words, or pixels among themselves, and then being able to predict the next one. If we step back and think about it, nearly every move we make, every moment of every single day, could be predicted by looking at what precedes it. If we break it down enough, is every single thing we do part of a sequence?

1.3 The Market

According to Research and Markets, the Generative AI market in North America is experiencing significant growth, with a projected compound annual growth rate (CAGR) of 31.4% from 2023 to 2028. As is usually the case with such early estimates, these may end up being off the mark, but compared to the same methodology applied to other market segments, one can clearly see that Generative AI is poised to experience very rapid growth. Verticals which will likely adopt this technology aggressively include Media & Entertainment, IT & Telecommunication, Healthcare, Automotive & Transportation, Legal, Energy, and Defense.

Generative AI enables many new business models and helps automate existing workflows. If leaders could generate text, graphics, video, audio, and music—and combinations thereof—how could they run their business better? Now add code and CAD designs. It's easy to see why the augmentation of expensive human labor represents such a massive opportunity.

Generative AI can be delivered via on-premise or cloud-hosted model. We'll discuss this further in the book and investigate why retaining control of important data is critical. The added effort to develop some internal application, service, and model hosting capacity is a worthwhile endeavor.

Unsurprisingly, the same Research and Markets report

indicates that the US market dominated the Generative AI market in North America and is expected to maintain its dominance until 2028, reaching a market value of $15 billion. The Canadian market is projected to grow at a CAGR of 34.4% during the forecast period (2022-2028), while the Mexican market is expected to witness a CAGR of 33.2% during the same period. The types of technologies that will drive this market include Transformers, Generative Adversarial Networks (GANs) and Variational Auto-encoders (VAEs), to name just a few generative mechanisms.

1.4   Why Should CEOs Care About Generative AI?

In today's evolving digital landscape, the question is not whether technology will transform the business world, but how disruptive this transformation will be. As CEOs navigate the labyrinth of emerging technologies, Generative AI presents the potential for innovation and immense financial opportunity. It is a journey that is simultaneously exhilarating and challenging, offering those willing to embrace it the potential to leapfrog the competition.

So, why should a CEO pay attention to Generative AI? The answer is multifold, rooted in the technology's unique ability to boost efficiency, spur innovation, and create competitive advantages. The AI revolution is unlike what has come before because it holds the potential to mechanize cognition. So far, humans have worked to build machines that can work faster, lift greater weight, and function for longer hours than any human can. In short, humans have replicated muscle. But now, we are at the cusp of being able to replicate mind—a singularly unique moment in our evolutionary history.

If you are an organizational leader thinking about Generative AI and wondering why you should take it seriously, let's examine just some of the many reasons why.

First, Generative AI can enhance productivity across various business functions. For instance, it can automate repetitive tasks, freeing up employees to focus on more complex and engaging work. A generative model can write reports, generate code, or even design websites, performing tasks in minutes that would otherwise take hours. Such capabilities can lead to significant time savings and improved operational efficiency.

Second, Generative AI can enhance decision making. AI models that can predict future scenarios or generate new ideas can provide fresh insights and perspectives. They can help leaders make informed decisions, minimizing risks and optimizing outcomes. For instance, generative models can simulate different business strategies and predict their outcomes, helping leaders choose the most promising path.

Third, Generative AI can spur innovation, opening new avenues for product and service development. It can generate creative solutions to problems, design new products, or create engaging content that would be difficult for a human to imagine, helping businesses stand out in a crowded market. For example, generative models are now being used to create unique fashion designs, write compelling marketing copy, or compose music for ads.

Further, Generative AI can enhance the customer experience. By generating hyper personalized content, recommendations, or responses, it can make interactions more relevant and engaging for customers. This can lead to increased customer satisfaction, loyalty, and ultimately, revenue.

The potential of Generative AI extends beyond immediate business applications. As the boundaries of AI expand, the technology is becoming a powerful tool for societal impact. It can generate educational content, contribute to scientific research, or create art, music, and literature, enriching our cultural heritage. Such applications can help businesses build a brand that resonates with values of creativity, innovation, and social impact.

However, as with any powerful technology, Generative AI brings its share of challenges. Issues of bias, security, and regulation loom large, demanding careful navigation. Leaders need to understand these challenges, as well as the moral implications of using Generative AI. It is their responsibility to ensure the technology is used in a manner that is ethical, fair, and beneficial for all stakeholders.

In the whirlwind of digital transformation, Generative AI stands out for its potential to reshape business and society. For CEOs, it offers an opportunity to lead this transformation—to harness the power of AI for the betterment of their organizations and the wider world. It is not just about staying ahead in the technology race; it is about shaping a future where technology serves humanity, supercharging our creativity and enriching our lives.

Embracing Generative AI is not merely a tactical move; it is a strategic decision that can redefine a business's trajectory. It requires foresight, courage, and a willingness to navigate the uncharted territories of technology. For those who dare, the rewards can be immense.

As we delve deeper into the world of Generative AI in the

following chapters, we will explore how leaders can harness its power, navigate its challenges, and shape its future. The journey is complex, but the destination is worth it—a world where human and machine creativity coexist and flourish, opening new horizons for innovation, growth, and societal impact.

CASE STUDY: Shell & SparkCognition Apply Generative AI to Oil Exploration

The oil and gas industry has faced numerous challenges over the past several years: logistics issues during COVID, the need to reduce environmental impact, and the ever-present requirement to continue to improve safety. Any technology that can make the process of exploration faster, easier, and cheaper contributes directly to all these goals, while massively impacting an energy company's top line.

It is in this context that the collaboration between Shell and SparkCognition provides a compelling case study. The effort aims to leverage Generative AI to drive forward a major shift in seismic exploration.

On May 16, 2023, a formal announcement from Austin, Texas, unveiled the technology collaboration between Spark-Cognition and Shell. The goal is to expedite the imaging and exploration of subsurface structures using Generative AI. Both firms are acutely aware of the need for increased efficiency in exploration workflows to ensure the possibility of heightened production and success rates. This partnership marked a commitment to that goal, employing advanced AI algorithms to process and analyze large quantities of data.

Traditional practices in subsurface imaging and data

analysis have long been arduous and costly. This approach demands vast amounts of data, high-performance computing, and complex physics-based algorithms. However, the Generative AI methodology promises a new way forward. This state-of-the-art technique uses deep learning to generate reliable subsurface images while significantly reducing the number of seismic shots needed, potentially as low as 1% of what is presently required, as proven in completed field trials. It is a clear demonstration of how AI can potentially improve established practices, leading to faster workflows and cost savings.

This collaboration aligns with Shell's larger digital transformation goals, a comprehensive plan to leverage the latest technologies to enhance operations. Gabriel Guerra, Vice President of Innovation & Performance at Shell, has been a major champion for this initiative and emphasizes the importance of innovative practices in exploration workflows as a critical step towards Shell's ambition. Working with Gabriel, Prof. Bruce Porter, Chief Science Officer at SparkCognition, believes that there is potential for Generative AI to disrupt traditional exploration practices, leading to potentially improved efficiencies and cost savings.

Both partner organizations have deep domain expertise in Energy. SparkCognition's Chairman, Lord John Browne, was the former CEO and Chairman of bp. His view of the importance of Generative AI for oil and gas is in context of the crucial role that the industry plays in the quest for a net-zero future. Browne underscores the importance of innovation to meet growing energy demands while reducing the industry's carbon footprint. This Generative AI initiative applies technology to sustainability by attempting to identify new reserves more efficiently.

This generative technology has applications far beyond oil and gas exploration. It can be applied to a wide array of complex problems where data and time reductions can have significant implications. These include on-shore exploration, satellite imaging for weather pattern prediction, national security, and threat assessment.

The Shell and SparkCognition collaboration represents a significant milestone in the field of oil and gas exploration. It offers a tangible example of how Generative AI, when applied thoughtfully and strategically, has the potential to revolutionize long-standing industry practices and delivering myriad financial, operational, and environmental benefits.

1.5   Chapter Summary

- Generative AI is a branch of artificial intelligence that focuses on creating new content, including text, images, music, and digital environments. It does this by learning from a dataset and generating new instances that share similar characteristics.

- Generative Adversarial Networks (GANs) and Transformer based models like GPT-3 and GPT-4 are leading examples of generative models. While GANs excel at image and music generation, Transformer-based models excel at text generation.

- Generative AI presents a novel canvas for creativity and problem solving. However, it requires substantial computational resources and training data, as well as a deep understanding of machine learning principles.

- Generative AI models, like GPT-3, operate on the principle of prediction, which extends beyond words to pixels and actions. By understanding the relationships among these elements, the model can predict the next element in the sequence.

- CEOs should pay attention to Generative AI due to its potential to boost efficiency, foster innovation, and create competitive advantages. It can enhance productivity, decision making, and customer experiences, as well as drive innovation and societal impact.

- Despite its potential, Generative AI presents challenges

around bias, security, and regulation. CEOs have a responsibility to ensure the ethical and fair use of the technology.

- Embracing Generative AI is a strategic decision that can redefine a business's trajectory, leading to innovation, growth, and societal impact.

1.6 Key Questions

1. What are the key differences between traditional machine learning models and generative models?

2. How do Generative Adversarial Networks (GANs) and Transformer-based models like GPT-3 and GPT-4 work, and what are their primary applications?

3. What is the principle of prediction in Generative AI, and how does it extend beyond words to pixels and actions?

4. How can Generative AI enhance productivity, decision making, and customer experiences in a business setting?

5. What are the potential societal impacts of Generative AI beyond immediate business applications?

6. What challenges does Generative AI present in terms of bias, security, and regulation, and how might these be addressed?

7. How can CEOs ensure the ethical and fair use of Generative AI in their organizations?

Chapter 2

The Benefits of Generative AI

2.1 Increased Productivity

Productivity is perhaps the most vital measure of any business operation, and this is precisely the area where Generative AI can offer substantial advantages. Generative AI extends far beyond simple automation. It doesn't merely perform tasks faster; it transforms the very nature of work, making tedious workflows that would be impossible to perform with manual labor, possible. For example, take the case of sifting through reams of documents looking for evidence. If the cost of legal analysts per hour, multiplied by the average number of hours it takes to find a claim, is greater than the average value of the claim, then the activity doesn't make economic sense. It is better to leave that money on the table, so to speak. But with Generative AI and Large Language Model (LLM) powered analysis, suddenly, what was uneconomic becomes possible and even downright inexpensive. The result is revenue from sources where the business didn't even care to look previously. Finding these types of opportunities can amplify earnings. In short, ideate, and let the LLMs figure out the rest.

Generative AI, with its ability to learn from existing data and create new content, also presents an opportunity to automate a variety of complex tasks which were previously considered solely in the human domain. Tasks that are routine, time consuming, or require substantial human effort can be automated and accomplished more efficiently, freeing up employees to focus on more strategic, complex, and creative aspects of their work. An example is double-checking process documentation to certify that key safety measures are stated in the documentation. In a typical business, perhaps a single human reading these documents must suffice to determine whether work logs indicate compliance. Any more than a single human reading, and it may mean taking a loss on a job, or impacting margins seriously. With LLMs, multiple AI systems can be guided (prompted) in different ways to automate analysis. What was complex and required domain expertise could be augmented with AI.

Let's take another example. Imagine a scenario where a content creation team is tasked with writing hundreds of product descriptions for an e-commerce platform. This is a task that demands time and human creativity. However, with Generative AI models, such as GPT-4, these descriptions can be written automatically, with creative flair, and in a fraction of the time it would take a human writer. The team can then focus on higher-level strategic planning or more complex creative challenges.

Further, consider the process of data analysis, which traditionally involves manual data collection, cleaning, analysis, and finally, the generation of reports. Each step is time-consuming and labor-intensive. However, Generative AI can automate parts of this process, such as generating insightful findings based on data patterns, reducing the time and effort needed, and enabling faster, more efficient decision making.

Another aspect of increased productivity through Generative AI lies in its ability to operate round-the-clock without fatigue or loss of efficiency. AI models can analyze vast amounts of data, generate reports, and perform tasks at any hour of the day or night. This non-stop operation can exponentially increase organizational productivity and output, especially in industries that require continuous operation, such as manufacturing, customer service, or IT support.

Generative AI's capacity to learn and improve over time lends itself to continuous productivity enhancement. As AI models learn from their interactions and feedback, they become more efficient and accurate, driving incremental productivity gains over time.

The benefits of Generative AI, however, are not merely about speed and efficiency. It is about quality, too. Generative AI models can generate high-quality outputs that match, and in some cases, surpass, human capabilities. Whether while creating a compelling piece of writing, designing a visually stunning graphic, or composing a piece of music, Generative AI can achieve a level of detail and creativity that enhances the quality of the product.

In the grand scheme of things, Generative AI's potential to increase productivity extends beyond individual tasks or processes. It can transform entire business models, industries, and economies, driving new levels of growth and prosperity. By automating routine tasks, enhancing decision making, and enabling new forms of creativity and innovation, Generative

AI can deliver quality at scale, catalyzing a productivity revolution that is set to redefine the future of work.

2.2 Improved Decision Making

One of the most significant benefits of Generative AI is the profound impact it has on decision-making processes. In a world where businesses generate vast amounts of data every day, the ability to derive valuable insights and make informed decisions is crucial. Generative AI can be a game-changer here, enhancing the quality, speed, and effectiveness of decision making at all levels of an organization.

Generative AI goes beyond traditional models which operate on rule-based systems, delivering binary (yes/no) outputs or pre-defined responses. Instead, it leverages deep learning algorithms to understand, learn, and generate new outputs, providing nuanced insights that can be instrumental in decision making.

The advantage of Generative AI in decision making is three-fold: data comprehension, predictive capabilities, and creativity in problem solving. Let's delve into each aspect to understand better how Generative AI can enhance decision-making processes.

2.2.1 Data Comprehension

Generative AI can analyze and comprehend vast amounts of data at a scale and speed far beyond human capability. It can identify patterns, trends, and correlations that might go unnoticed by human analysts. This ability to make sense of complex, unstructured data can provide leaders with deeper insights, enabling them to make better-informed decisions. For instance, an LLM can analyze customer reviews, social media posts, and online discussions to derive insights about customer sentiment and preferences, guiding product development and marketing strategies.

2.2.2 Predictive Capabilities

LLMs, once fine-tuned with enterprise data, can make accurate predictions about future outcomes based on historical data. For example, they can forecast sales trends, predict customer behavior, or anticipate market changes. These predictive capabilities can be invaluable in strategic planning, risk management, and resource allocation, enabling leaders to make proactive, data-driven decisions.

2.2.3 Creativity in Problem Solving

Generative AI can propose a variety of potential solutions for a given problem or task. This creative problem-solving capability can aid in decision making by providing diverse options and perspectives, fostering innovative thinking, and challenging conventional wisdom. Think of those brainstorming sessions guided by a consultant costing thousands of dollars an hour. Where do they all start? By people placing their ideas on the board, or on sticky notes placed on the wall. That type of ideation comes at machine speed with LLMs. For instance, a Generative AI model can propose multiple strategic options for business expansion, each with its pros and cons based on data analysis, allowing leaders to weigh different approaches and make the best decision.

Generative AI can also contribute to collective decision-making processes by facilitating collaboration and consensus-building. AI models can collate and analyze diverse viewpoints, identify commonalities and differences, and generate a range of balanced, data-informed proposals for consideration. This can help to streamline decision making in large, complex organizations, making it more inclusive, transparent, and effective.

If technology is used the right way, it can help mitigate the impact of cognitive biases in decision making. Humans are prone to a range of cognitive biases that can distort their judgment and decision making. Generative AI models, if properly designed and trained, can provide a more objective, data-driven perspective, helping to counteract these biases and improve the quality of decisions.

Generative AI definitely has the potential to enhance decision making, but like everything else, it is not a magic bullet. The quality of AI-generated insights and decisions remains heavily dependent on the quality of the data it learns from, the fine-tuning processes it is subjected to, and the prompts used to create output. It is crucial for organizations to ensure their data is accurate, comprehensive, and unbiased.

Decisions made by Generative AI should, for now, be subject to human oversight and judgment. AI models, for all their sophistication, don't possess human intuition, ethical judgment, or contextual understanding. There remains a non-zero risk that over-reliance on AI could lead to poor decisions or unintended consequences. Ultimately, all organizations should be held responsible for the technology they deploy, including AI they develop or anything they develop with AI.

2.3   New Product and Service Development

In an era where market dynamics are continuously evolving and competitors are iterating on the order of days and weeks, the ability to innovate and develop new products and services is a critical determinant of an organization's success. Generative AI has the potential to accelerate this process, providing a powerful tool for innovation and creativity. Its capabilities can be harnessed in numerous ways to support new product and service development. In this section, we will explore these opportunities, diving into the role of Generative AI in ideation, design, prototyping, testing, and customization.

2.3.1   Ideation

The generation of new ideas is the first step in product or service development. Generative AI can stimulate creativity and expand the ideation process by suggesting novel concepts or combinations that might not have been considered otherwise. For example, AI can analyze data on consumer trends, market dynamics, and competitive offerings to propose potential product ideas. It can also identify gaps in the market that could be filled by new products or services.

2.3.2   Design

Generative AI can play a major role in product design. AI algorithms can generate multiple design options based on specified parameters, allowing designers to explore a wide range of possibilities quickly. For instance, generative design tools can create numerous variations of a product component, each optimized for different factors like strength, weight, cost, or sustainability. Designers can then choose the best options or iterate further based on these outputs.

2.3.3 Prototyping

AI can also speed up the prototyping process. With generative models, businesses can create virtual prototypes and simulate their performance under various conditions, reducing the time and cost of physical prototyping. For example, AI can simulate how a new car model will perform in different weather conditions or how a new building design will stand up to various stress factors.

2.3.4 Testing

Generative AI can generate synthetic data to augment testing and validation processes. This can be especially valuable when actual data is scarce, sensitive, or expensive to collect. For instance, AI can generate synthetic user profiles to test a new app, ensuring it works well for a wide range of user types and scenarios.

2.3.5 Customization

Perhaps one of the most exciting applications of Generative AI is in product customization. AI can generate personalized product recommendations or custom designs based on individual customer preferences, providing a highly tailored customer experience. For example, an AI model could design a custom piece of furniture based on a customer's preferred style, space constraints, and budget.

2.3.6   Programming with LLMs

Programming talent is now some of the most expensive to hire and retain. Many large companies spend dozens and hundreds of millions of dollars a year maintaining teams that can write and customize software. Making these teams more productive and allowing less experienced developers to be more efficient would present massive economic opportunities for business.

The UNIX operating system, developed in the 1960s and 1970s, offered a multi-user, interactive computing model which represented a profound shift in the world of computer science and programming. UNIX was designed to share a powerful computer system among multiple users, facilitating interactive computing. However, the true value of UNIX extended far beyond its technical contributions. UNIX was built on a profound philosophy aptly named the "UNIX philosophy." One of its key tenets was: "Do one thing and do it well."

In UNIX, specialized programs designed to perform specific tasks took text as input and produced text as output. These small, specialized programs could then be linked, or "composed" in a process known as "composability." The "pipe" was the composability operator on the UNIX command line, enabling the combination of individual programs. For instance, on the command line, a user could use the *cat* command to display the contents of a file. This output could then be piped into another program such as *nl*, which counted the number of lines. The genius of this system was its loose coupling and its ability to combine small programs dynamically to execute more complex tasks.

In the current era, we're witnessing a similar revolution with the advent of language models. These models not only comprehend free form text but also understand technical and API documentation. They enable us to apply the UNIX philosophy to dynamically create applications. Here, the "chains" are empowered through the use of Large Language Models (LLMs) , which dynamically link APIs to resolve complex problems.

There are three aspects to this that are worth a deep dive.

First, an LLM is a remarkable partner for task description and problem solving. For instance, a user can instruct the LLM: "You are an LLM that multiplies. The only two functions you have are 'add' and 'run x times.'" The LLM is then capable of figuring out that, by repeatedly adding a number, it can simulate multiplication. This demonstrates the LLM's ability to derive higher-level functions from the provided primitives and to comprehend how to interconnect these elements. This makes an LLM a text-programmable "computer."

Second, consider a more complex scenario where the API retrieves data, processes it into a data frame, and applies various analytical tools like charting capabilities or clustering algorithms. Adhering to the UNIX philosophy of using a loosely coupled interim data format helps avoid potential issues when connecting these modules together. With LLMs acting as the glue, we can describe problems that can be solved by combining individual atomic elements of an API. This approach enables us to weave together an entire application using LLMs, chaining them with API calls.

This emerging pattern in software engineering veers away from the traditional strongly-typed programming methods that require a class to implement a specific interface. Instead, it introduces a more loosely coupled approach where LLMs creatively combine API calls and local command-line tools to solve problems. LLMs can determine the sequence of operations, and experience leads to the conclusion that they've shown a capability to combine component parts effectively to build a full application.

In essence, this method of deploying LLMs represents the AI iteration of the UNIX philosophy. Here, simple components that perform one task well are combined, not with UNIX command line pipes, but with cognitively capable LLMs. This approach could fundamentally alter software development, as the composability is dynamic and refactoring of components is near real-time.

Lastly, the output of every LLM is text, which is interpretable by any other LLM. Much like text is the standard data type passed between individual programs on the UNIX command line, so it is with LLMs. But in this case, no hard-coded formats are necessary. Highly specific functionality can be applied to data that is loosely, if at all, formatted.

When all this is put together, a new software development paradigm emerges. A new text description can quickly alter the entire program, including selecting different API calls and tools. While the thought of debugging such a system might seem daunting, LLM-powered debuggers and test case writers can come to the rescue. As this new software development paradigm evolves, best practices and innovative techniques will undoubtedly emerge.

The potential of LLMs as a software development tool is immense, serving as both the glue that binds various components and the embodiment of the UNIX philosophy. It may be worthwhile for any and all programmers intrigued by these ideas to experiment with this approach, set up basic tests, and explore the tremendous potential that LLMs offer.

2.3.7 Final Thoughts on New Product and Service Development

The potential of Generative AI in new product and service development is vast. However, it is not without its challenges. As with any AI application, the outputs of Generative AI are only as good as the data it learns from. Ensuring the quality, diversity, and fairness of this data is crucial. There are also important ethical considerations around the use of AI in product development, particularly when it comes to personalization and data privacy.

Moreover, while Generative AI can support and augment human creativity, it can't yet replace it entirely. The intuitive leaps, contextual understanding, and ethical judgment that humans bring to product development are beyond the reach of current AI technologies. Therefore, a successful AI-driven product development strategy (at least one developed in 2023!) should aim to augment human creativity, not replace it.

In the next sections, we will explore how to integrate

Generative AI into your organization effectively and discuss the broader implications of this technology for the future of leadership and business.

CASE STUDY: Airbus uses Generative AI to design aircraft

As sustainability and eco-friendly approaches become the cornerstone of technological advancements worldwide, the aviation industry is not to be left behind. Pioneering the path is Airbus, championing the use of generative design and 3D printing to completely transform the future of air travel.

The vision of Airbus is not just a change, it is a revolution. The dream is to make air travel a dynamic, eco-friendly experience, curated to perfection by the ambitious and innovative minds at Airbus's Emerging Technologies and Concepts group in Germany. Under the leadership of Innovation Manager Bastian Schaefer, the team is tirelessly working towards building aircraft that are not only efficient but also comfortable in a myriad of ways. From creating spaces that allow passengers to work, play, and collaborate, to ensuring more privacy and room, Airbus is pushing the boundaries of conventional air travel.

An embodiment of this futuristic vision is the Airbus Concept Plane. With an aim to provide a highly customized flying experience and a strong commitment to eco-friendliness, Airbus has leveraged the power of generative design. This groundbreaking technology mimics nature's evolutionary design process, discovering optimal solutions through extensive exploration and learning.

The technology, underpinned by cloud computing, cycles through thousands or even millions of design possibilities, testing configurations and learning from each iteration. The result? A solution far superior and innovative than what a human mind could conceive independently.

One of the earliest practical applications of generative design at Airbus was the development of a new cabin partition for the Airbus A320. Termed the "bionic partition," this structure boasted of being lighter, stronger, and thinner than its predecessor, while also fulfilling stringent requirements for weight, stress, and displacement during a crash scenario. The design process was guided by algorithms inspired by the growth patterns of slime mold and mammal bones—biomimicry at its finest—resulting in an optimized latticed structure.

3D printing, another revolutionary technology, was instrumental in the realization of the bionic partition. Over 100 separate pieces of this high-strength metal alloy partition were 3D printed and assembled, marking the creation of the world's largest 3D-printed aircraft cabin component.

The implications of the bionic partition extend beyond innovative design, touching the realm of environmental sustainability. Each bionic partition saves a whopping 3,180 kg of jet fuel per year, thus reducing CO_2 emissions substantially. If the entire Airbus A320 were to be fitted with these partitions, the weight reduction could be up to 500 kg, equating to an annual decrease of up to 166 metric tons of CO_2 emissions per aircraft. Moreover, 3D printing uses only a fraction of the raw material required for traditional milling, with the majority of leftover material being recyclable.

The triumph of the bionic partition project has opened new avenues for Airbus to apply generative design and 3D printing to more areas of aircraft manufacturing. Larger structures within planes, such as the cockpit wall or galley structure, are being considered for a similar design overhaul. However, realizing this ambitious vision will necessitate the development of bigger, faster 3D printers and a workforce adept in these novel design and production methodologies.

In this era of sustainable innovation, generative design and 3D printing are poised to play pivotal roles in reshaping the aviation industry. The journey of Airbus and its bionic partition project stands as a testament to the transformative potential of these technologies—revolutionizing design, manufacturing, and the environmental footprint of air travel.

2.4 Enhanced Customer Experiences

The customer experience is the sum of all interactions a customer has with a company, from first learning about the company to using products or services offered. It is the holistic perception developed during this cycle of interaction that can significantly influence a customer's satisfaction and loyalty. With the rise of Generative AI, businesses have an unprecedented opportunity to elevate the customer experience in multiple dimensions.

2.4.1 Hyper Personalization

One of the most compelling applications of Generative AI is in hyper personalization. AI algorithms can analyze a vast array of data, from purchase history to browsing behavior, to understand individual customer preferences and behaviors. This insight can be used to personalize everything from product recommendations to marketing messages, creating a highly tailored customer experience that increases engagement and loyalty. Companies can literally field a conversational system that is a singular expert in understanding and catering to the user's needs and desires.

2.4.2 Customer Support

AI can also improve the customer support experience. Generative AI models, such as chatbots or virtual assistants, can provide instant, 24/7 support, answering common queries, guiding customers through troubleshooting steps, or even assisting with product setup or usage. These models learn from each interaction, continually improving their ability to understand and respond to customer needs. One of the additional technologies companies should investigate with their implementation partners if they go down this road is ring-fencing—limiting the LLM to answer questions that are appropriate to answer and not allowing conversations to morph into general purpose dialogue, or improper exchanges.

2.4.3 Seamless Interactions

Generative AI can help create seamless, frictionless customer interactions. For example, AI can generate personalized user interfaces that adapt to individual user habits or needs, making it easier for customers to navigate websites or apps, find information, or complete transactions. AI can also automate routine tasks, like form filling or appointment scheduling, saving customers time and effort.

2.4.4 Predictive Services

By analyzing patterns in customer behavior, AI can anticipate customer needs and provide services proactively. For example, a subscription service could use AI to predict when a customer is likely to run out of a product and offer a timely refill. Or an always-alive AI process could identify when a customer is likely to need support, based on their usage patterns, and provide proactive assistance.

2.4.5 Experiential Marketing

Generative AI can create immersive, interactive experiences that engage customers in novel ways. For instance, AI could generate virtual reality environments for product demonstrations or simulations, allowing customers to experience a product virtually before they buy. Or AI could create personalized content, like stories, games, or interactive videos, that engage customers with a brand in a more meaningful, memorable way.

Undoubtedly, tantalizing levels of personalization are possible with LLMs, but these programs must be balanced with user privacy concerns. Businesses must ensure they handle customer data responsibly. Customer support AI must be designed with empathy and cultural sensitivity in mind, to provide support that is not only efficient but also respectful and human-centered.

Seamless interactions and predictive services must be built on a deep understanding of customer behavior, which requires not only sophisticated AI but also a comprehensive, integrated view of customer data. Many businesses struggle with data silos that hinder this kind of holistic understanding.

While AI can create unique, engaging experiences, it must do so in a way that is authentic and consistent with the brand. AI-generated content or experiences that feel artificial or off-brand can detract from the customer experience rather than enhancing it.

In the next chapter, we will delve into the challenges of Generative AI in greater detail and discuss strategies for overcoming them. The future of customer experience is exciting, but it requires thoughtful, strategic leadership to navigate successfully.

2.5 Chapter Summary

- Generative AI has significant potential in enhancing business operations, particularly in the realms of productivity, decision making, and new product or service development.

- In the realm of productivity, Generative AI can automate complex tasks, transform workflows, and find new revenue sources, thus amplifying human productivity.

- Generative AI greatly improves decision-making processes through data comprehension, predictive capabilities, and creativity in problem solving, allowing for better-informed, proactive, and innovative decisions.

- Generative AI plays a pivotal role in new product and service development, aiding in ideation, design, prototyping, testing, and customization, thus accelerating innovation and customer personalization.

- Generative AI can stimulate creativity in ideation, generate multiple design options, speed up prototyping, augment testing with synthetic data, and create personalized product recommendations or custom designs.

- LLMs (Large Language Models) can revolutionize software development, acting as the glue that dynamically links APIs to resolve complex problems. This new paradigm represents the AI iteration of the UNIX philosophy.

- The quality of Generative AI outputs relies heavily on the quality, diversity, and fairness of the data it learns from. Ethical considerations around AI use in product development, particularly in terms of personalization and data privacy, are paramount.

2.6 Key Questions

1. How can Generative AI significantly enhance productivity within a business? Provide examples.

2. What are the three main ways in which Generative AI improves decision-making processes?

3. Discuss how Generative AI can revolutionize new product and service development. What are the key areas of this process where AI can have a significant impact?

4. Explain the role of LLMs in software development. How does this represent an AI iteration of the UNIX philosophy?

5. What are the key challenges and ethical considerations when implementing Generative AI in business operations, particularly in new product and service development?

6. How does Generative AI's ability to comprehend vast amounts of data affect decision making in businesses?

7. How can Generative AI contribute to collective decision-making processes within large, complex organizations?

Chapter 3

The Challenges of Generative AI

3.1 Bias

As we navigate the promises of Generative AI, it is crucial to address an inherent challenge: bias. The subject of bias in AI has grown into a focal area of concern for organizations worldwide, and for good reasons. Bias in Generative AI systems can lead to discriminatory results, causing harm to customers while tarnishing brand reputation and potentially leading to regulatory repercussions.

3.1.1 What is AI Bias?

AI bias can be understood as systemic prejudice in AI outputs, often due to underlying bias in training data or algorithms. For instance, if an AI is trained on data reflecting historical inequalities or prejudices, it can perpetuate or even exacerbate these biases in its outputs. This problem is compounded by the fact that bias can be subtle and hard to detect without careful analysis.

Tackling the "White Obama" Bias

AI researchers across the globe are working hard to refine models, improve accuracy, and eliminate bias. But this can be a daunting task. In a recent lecture at the Machine Learning Lab at the University of Texas at Austin, a particular case stood out.

In a special public lecture titled, "AI for Accurate and Fair Imaging," a team from the Institute for Foundations of Machine Learning (IFML), housed within the lab, unveiled their work on bias elimination. Their mission? To tweak the algorithm that sparked internet fame with an image transformation of former President Barack Obama into a white man, the so-called "White Obama."

In 2020, an AI model was designed to refine a pixelated, low-resolution snapshot of Obama. However, the outcome was a stark transformation, a result that Alex Dimakis, the IFML co-director, identified as bias. "Despite producing a high resolution, realistic human image, the bias was evident," he explained.

Embarking on the mission to improve the technology, Dimakis and his team first suspected the training data used for the algorithm—a collection largely composed of white celebrities. But the true culprit soon revealed itself—the structure of the algorithm. "The algorithm's focus on getting the correct answer resulted in the magnification of even minimal bias in the dataset," Dimakis noted.

The algorithm's imperfections stretched beyond racial aspects. Another enhanced photo incorrectly depicted a turban as hair, hinting at its potential to foster discrimination. "The algorithm can indeed be very discriminatory," echoed Adam Klivans, the co-director of IFML.

However, Klivans shed light on the brighter side of improving AI accuracy. It extends its reach beyond issues of race and gender to other realms, including medical imaging. This advancement could offer doctors high-quality images for review.

The researchers at the Machine Learning Lab, through their groundbreaking work, aim to develop AI technology that is both accurate and fair. Their pursuit serves as a testament to the need for ongoing refinement of AI algorithms, ensuring that they fulfill their purpose without inadvertently introducing bias.

3.1.2 The Impact of Bias in Generative AI

Bias can manifest in Generative AI in various ways. For example, an AI model trained on text data might generate text that reflects gender stereotypes if the training data included such biases. Similarly, a Generative AI system used for hiring might discriminate against certain groups if it is trained on data reflecting historical hiring biases.

The ramifications of these biases can be severe. They can lead to unfair outcomes, such as the exclusion of qualified candidates in hiring or the perpetuation of harmful stereotypes in marketing content. They can also harm a company's reputation and expose it to legal and regulatory risks.

3.1.3 Addressing Bias

Addressing bias in Generative AI requires a multifaceted

approach. Here are some strategies:

- **Diverse and representative data:** Ensuring the data used to train AI systems is diverse and representative can help mitigate bias. This might involve gathering more data from underrepresented groups or weighting the data to reflect the diversity of the population accurately.

- **Bias detection and mitigation algorithms:** Several techniques can help detect and mitigate bias in AI models. For instance, fairness metrics can quantify bias in AI outputs, while debiasing algorithms can adjust AI models to reduce bias.

- **Extensive testing:** Particularly for systems that are customer facing, there can never be enough testing. Alpha and beta launches that deliver functionality to a small set of testers and potential customers are essential for major AI-enabled products.

3.1.4 Interpretability

Making AI systems more transparent and interpretable can help stakeholders understand how AI makes decisions and where bias might be creeping in. This can involve using explainable AI techniques or opening up the "black box" of AI with tools like feature importance maps or saliency maps.

- **Ethical guidelines and oversight:** Establishing clear ethical guidelines for AI use and setting up independent oversight bodies can help prevent and detect bias. These measures can also ensure accountability and foster trust among stakeholders.

- **Inclusive design and testing:** Including diverse perspectives in the AI development process and testing AI systems with diverse user groups can help identify and address bias. This can involve diverse development teams or user testing with representative user groups.

- **Regulation and standards:** Complying with existing regulations and standards related to AI bias, and advocating for the development of clear, fair standards can also help tackle this issue.

Addressing bias in Generative AI is not just an ethical imperative but also a business need. By proactively addressing bias, organizations can build fairer, more trustworthy AI systems that deliver better results for all users, enhancing brand reputation and mitigating regulatory risks. The journey towards bias-free AI might be complex, but it is one that enterprises cannot afford to overlook.

3.2 Security

Generative AI, as with any technology, has its vulnerabilities. One of the most significant is its susceptibility to cyber-physical attacks. The introduction of Generative AI into a company's business ecosystem, while providing many benefits, also opens new doors for potential threats. Understanding these threats, and more importantly, how to mitigate them, is crucial in maintaining the integrity of a business.

3.2.1 Security Challenges of Generative AI

One prominent security concern with Generative AI is its potential misuse. The technology's ability to generate human-like text, audio, and video can be exploited to create deepfakes, disinformation, or automated phishing attacks, leading to serious implications for individuals and organizations alike. Moreover, the AI models themselves are targets for attacks.

Adversarial attacks, for instance, involve feeding deceptive input into the system to fool it into making incorrect predictions. These attacks can have serious consequences, particularly in critical applications like cybersecurity or healthcare. It is important to note that these attacks can be cyber in nature, where input sequences such as digital images are modified to include adversarial inputs, or physical in nature, where adversarial images or drawings are created in the physical world to confuse, for example, a self-driving car. Let's study this example in a bit more detail.

While the advent of self-driving cars seems imminent, a critical question lingers. Can these AI-driven machines navigate the complexity of our roads and react aptly to any kind of unexpected scenario? In fact, experiments have shown that the deep learning image classification systems used by many self-driving cars, despite their sophistication, are susceptible to adversarial attacks. Perpetrators can subtly manipulate an image, adding an almost imperceptible layer of noise, which can lead the system to grossly misinterpret it. This vulnerability is a cause for concern, considering these systems constitute the core functioning units of self-driving cars. Physical adversarial attacks against cars involve tampering with the actual environment. One prevalent method is altering road signs to mislead the car's AI system while remaining perfectly comprehensible to humans. This form of attack is not only more feasible but has also been shown to succeed in real-world scenarios. A research paper titled, "Robust Physical-World Attacks on Deep Learning Visual Classification," written by researchers at The University of California at Berkeley, The University of Michigan at Ann Arbor, and The University of Washington, found that physical adversarial attacks caused an incorrect image label to be induced over 84% of the time.

Despite these issues, there is hope. One strategy to counter these attacks is to develop machine learning systems robust enough to identify adversarial examples. This could be achieved through extensive training and repeated exposure to adversarial methods, thereby enhancing the system's resilience. Another possible approach is to adopt redundancy within the car's control system. By using ancillary systems, like GPS, to corroborate the decisions made by the deep learning system, an extra layer of validation can be added.

3.2.2 Mitigating Security Risks

Addressing these security risks involves a combination of technical and procedural measures:

- **Robust Model Design and Testing:** By employing robust AI techniques, models can be made more resistant to adversarial attacks. Testing models under different attack scenarios can also help identify vulnerabilities and devise countermeasures.

- **Secure Data Management:** Implementing stringent data governance policies can help protect sensitive data. This includes de-identifying data, using secure data storage and transfer methods, and monitoring access to data.

- **User Education:** Users need to be aware of the potential risks associated with Generative AI and how to identify and report suspicious activity. Regular training and awareness campaigns can help achieve this.

- **Ethics and Policies:** Establishing clear guidelines on the ethical use of Generative AI can help prevent misuse. This could include guidelines on data usage, model deployment, and incident response.

- **Regulatory Compliance:** Complying with relevant laws and regulations can also help mitigate risks. This could involve data protection laws, AI regulations, or sector-specific rules.

- **Collaboration:** Collaborating with other organizations, industry bodies, and regulators can help keep abreast of the latest threats and best practices. This could involve participating in information-sharing platforms, contributing to standards development, or engaging in joint research initiatives.

The US Department of Defense on Generative AI: Full Speed Ahead!

Generative AI is fast becoming a hot topic in the defense industry. While there have been calls to slow down this research, a markedly different perspective arises from the Department of Defense (DoD). Its leaders view the technology as a force multiplier and essential to staying ahead in an increasingly digital battlefield.

As emphasized by Lt. Gen Robert Skinner, Director of the Defense Information Systems Agency (DISA), a halt in Generative AI research is not an option. This perspective was shared during the AFCEA TechNet Cyber conference in Baltimore, where DoD leaders gathered to discuss AI's potential, including promising models like OpenAI's GPT-3 and Google's Bard. Skinner asserted that pausing Generative AI research would be a tactical misstep, as their adversaries certainly would not. The focus of Generative AI, according to Skinner, goes beyond merely thwarting U.S. adversaries. He sees the technology as an empowerment tool, even for those with less expertise, to develop malware and other capabilities. In other words, Generative AI is a game-changer, bringing unprecedented benefits and challenges alike.

Skinner's call to industry is loud and clear: help is needed to figure out the best way to leverage this technology for safety and protection. This isn't a battle; it's a race to find who can best utilize Generative AI. It's a journey into a new realm of technology that demands cooperation, innovation, and vigilance.

According to Stephen Wallace, DISA's director of emerging technologies, the real strength of AI lies not merely in the technology itself, but in the authenticity of the underlying data. He compared the current state of Generative AI to the early days of the internet when the potential impacts were yet to be fully understood. However, he predicts Generative

AI will outpace the internet's growth and evolution.

Wallace sees Generative AI as an invaluable tool for tasks such as data tagging and labeling, and most importantly, as a force multiplier for their team. This technology, he stated, is an augmentation tool for making their teams more efficient and effective, ultimately enhancing capabilities across the board.

3.2.3   The Role of Leadership

The onus is on leaders to ensure that their organizations take a proactive stance on Generative AI security. This means fostering a culture of security awareness, investing in secure AI development practices, partnering with AI technology firms that understand these challenges deeply, and working closely with internal and external stakeholders to address security concerns.

Generative AI presents immense opportunities for businesses, but it also brings with it new security challenges. By understanding these risks and taking steps to mitigate them, leaders can ensure that their organizations reap the benefits of Generative AI while safeguarding against the downsides.

Engaging the Team: A Letter from the CEO

Dear Team,

Generative AI is changing our industry, and we must leverage it everywhere we can. This is one of those technological advancements that comes about rarely but reshapes the environment in massive ways. It is simple: the acceleration that generative tools offer us makes them an imperative. The only choice here is to adopt or fall behind. I am writing to let you know that we are launching a company-wide effort to systematically adopt Generative AI to help us improve quality, productivity, and efficiency.

Overview

Every department has been tasked with exploring ways to use Generative AI technology to improve operational efficiency. Generative tools can enhance operational efficiency by automating repetitive tasks and allowing teams to focus on core operations. They can streamline administrative and technical tasks, automating everything from scheduling and composing emails to summarizing code and generating reports.

If we successfully harness these tools, we can easily achieve our productivity and efficiency targets for this year. We can pass along efficiencies through our product offerings to our customers so they can also benefit. Not optimizing these practices puts us at risk of missing our company and personal goals and losing business to competitors.

Timeline

We will distribute a formal policy to establish guidelines for appropriate use of AI tools by everyone associated with our organization and its subsidiaries. Internal teams are testing customized and locally hosted Large Language Models (LLMs) and Image Generation Applications that can be utilized with both external and internal data. Below is an overview of the timeline:

- Policy for Appropriate Use of AI Tools (week of dd/mm/yy)

- Create, test, and deploy our Jarvis LLM (V1 launch dd/mm/yy)

- Create, test, and deploy our Code Bear LLM (V1 launch dd/mm/yy)

Enablement

We will organize workshops and create training videos to assist you in learning more about Generative AI technology. Below are examples of some of our plans:

- Workshops by function
- Workshops for general education on Generative AI from internal AI experts
- Produce 10-minute training videos accessible to all company employees

You are encouraged to use Generative AI technology throughout the business including, but not limited to:

- Composing emails, interpreting legal contracts, writing reports
- Creating marketing posters, road mapping ideation, website graphics, entire document/HTML layouts, landing pages, creating copy, SEO optimizing existing content
- Analyzing code, debugging code, writing code, writing IT scripts and automations

- Writing job descriptions, summarizing, and auto comparing resumes

- Writing test cases, writing and optimizing marketing content, preliminary data analysis, and summarization

- Summarizing financial accounts, generating tabular projections for Excel, creating investor updates, summarizing documents for due diligence

Generative AI Implementation and Measurement

We have established the Generative AI Implementation Group with diverse perspectives across the company to encourage cross-collaboration and provide guidance and support. They will also capture best practices and lessons learned to find use cases that can overlap between departments. The group will help ensure that stakeholders are aware of improvements through the use of AI tools aligned with the company's goals for 2023. The Operations team will organize meetings to discuss how AI tools are being utilized to drive productivity and efficiency throughout the year.

Please contact your manager or me directly if you have any questions or need initial training.

Best regards,
Amir

3.3 Regulation

Generative AI, like any disruptive technology, is a frontier where regulation is still evolving. Understanding the regulatory landscape and its implications for an organization is crucial. This section delves into the perplexing world of AI regulation and how it can integrate into a business strategy, shaping the decisions leaders make about adopting Generative AI.

3.3.1   Regulatory Landscapes

Regulation of AI is a complex issue due to its global nature, rapid development, and broad applications. Different countries have varying levels of regulation, ranging from comprehensive legal frameworks to more laissez-faire approaches.

In the European Union, for instance, draft regulations propose a risk-based approach, with stricter rules for "high-risk" AI applications. In contrast, the United States has been more industry-friendly, promoting voluntary standards and sector-specific guidelines. However, regulation in the United States is surely coming.

3.3.2   Regulation Areas

The major areas of AI regulation include transparency, fairness, privacy, and accountability. Transparency requires AI systems to be explainable and their decision-making processes understandable to users. Fairness ensures AI does not discriminate or perpetuate biases. Privacy regulations aim to protect the vast amounts of data used in AI training, while accountability involves establishing who is responsible when AI systems go wrong.

3.3.3   Implications for Businesses

These emerging regulations have profound implications for businesses. Firstly, they can lead to increased costs and complexity in AI development and deployment. Leaders may need to invest more in ensuring their AI systems are transparent, fair, and secure, and in demonstrating compliance with regulations.

Secondly, they can affect strategic decisions about AI. Leaders may need to consider regulatory risks when deciding which AI applications to pursue, where to deploy them, and how to design and manage them.

Thirdly, they can impact a company's relationships with customers, partners, and stakeholders. Compliance with AI regulations can enhance a company's reputation and build trust, while noncompliance can damage a brand and lead to legal and financial penalties.

3.3.4 Navigating the Regulatory Maze

How can leaders navigate this regulatory maze? Here are some pointers:

- **Stay Informed:** Keep abreast of the latest regulatory developments in your jurisdiction and industry. This may involve working with legal and regulatory experts, joining industry associations, or participating in regulatory consultations.

- **Embed Compliance:** Integrate regulatory compliance into your AI strategy and operations. This could involve developing policies and procedures, providing training, and establishing mechanisms for monitoring and reporting compliance.

- **Engage with Regulators:** Engage proactively with regulators to understand their expectations, share your perspectives, and influence regulatory development. This can be beneficial for both parties, as regulators gain industry insights and you are able to anticipate regulatory changes.

- **Build Ethical AI:** Strive to build AI systems that are not only legally compliant, but also ethical. This involves going beyond minimum regulatory requirements to ensure your AI systems are transparent, fair, secure, and beneficial for society.

3.3.5   The Future of AI Regulation

The future of AI regulation is uncertain and likely to be shaped by many factors, including technological advances, societal attitudes, and political considerations. But if a company is serious about implementing Generative AI, then it is vital to anticipate these changes, adapt strategies, and help shape the regulatory environment to support beneficial and responsible use of Generative AI.

One example where clarity in regulation and certification is needed in order for the sector to make progress is aviation. Currently, neural network-based systems that control aircraft are unlikely to meet FAA (Federal Aviation Administration) certification requirements in the United States. In this area, in particular, it remains to be seen how quickly regulatory authorities can adapt to the new reality of the AI era.

While AI regulation can be complex and challenging, it also provides an opportunity for businesses to demonstrate their commitment to responsible AI, build trust with stake-holders, and gain a competitive edge in the rapidly evolving AI landscape. If companies get ahead of these coming changes and lean in, perhaps even to work with government officials developing regulation, they can not only help shape the future, but also represent their customers' interests more effectively. Such leadership never goes unnoticed.

3.4 Chapter Summary

- Bias in Generative AI can lead to discriminatory outputs that could damage a brand's reputation and potentially have legal consequences.

- Bias in AI refers to systemic prejudice in the outputs of AI, often due to bias in training data or algorithms, which can perpetuate or exacerbate historical inequalities or prejudices.

- Addressing bias in Generative AI is challenging but essential, as illustrated by the "White Obama" case from the Machine Learning Lab at the University of Texas at Austin.

- Bias can manifest in different ways in Generative AI, such as reflecting gender stereotypes or discriminating against certain groups in a hiring process, if the training data includes such biases.

- Strategies to address bias include ensuring diverse and representative data, employing bias detection and mitigation algorithms, making AI systems more transparent and interpretable, setting ethical guidelines and oversight, inclusive design and testing, and adhering to regulation and standards.

- The security vulnerabilities of Generative AI include potential for misuse in creating deepfakes or carrying out phishing attacks.

- Leaders have a crucial role in promoting a security-conscious culture and investing in secure AI practices.

- AI regulation, covering transparency, fairness, privacy, and accountability, has significant implications for businesses, impacting development costs, strategic decisions, and stakeholder relationships.

- Leaders can navigate the regulatory landscape by staying informed, embedding compliance into AI strategy and operations, engaging with regulators, and building ethical AI systems.

3.5   Key Questions

1. What is AI bias and how can it manifest in Generative AI systems?

2. How did the "White Obama" case illustrate the challenge of bias in AI? What were the key learnings from this case?

3. What strategies can be used to address bias in Generative AI?

4. What are the potential security vulnerabilities associated with Generative AI?

5. What role should leaders play in ensuring Generative AI security?

6. What are the main areas of AI regulation, and how might they impact businesses?

7. How can leaders effectively navigate the complex regulatory landscape surrounding AI?

Chapter 4

Adopting Generative AI

4.1 Develop a Generative AI Strategy

Establishing a robust and comprehensive strategy is a critical first step for organizations venturing into the world of Generative AI. This complex and dynamic process involves critical decisions and deep analysis. In this section, we will discuss the elements that should be considered when formulating a Generative AI strategy.

4.1.1 Understanding Your Business Context

An effective Generative AI strategy begins with a clear understanding of your business context. This involves assessing your organization's strengths, weaknesses, opportunities, and threats (SWOT), and identifying the areas where Generative AI can add the most value. It might be in enhancing productivity, improving decision making, developing new products and services, or enhancing customer experience.

4.1.2 Defining Your AI Vision and Goals

Your Generative AI strategy should be guided by a clear vision and set of goals. What do you want to achieve with Generative AI? How does it align with your overall business strategy and objectives? Having a clear vision and goals not only gives direction to your AI efforts, but also helps to gain buy-in from stakeholders and to measure progress and success.

4.1.3   Assessing Your AI Capabilities

An honest assessment of your current AI capabilities is crucial in developing your strategy. This involves evaluating your data infrastructure, technological resources, and human capabilities. Do you have the right data to train your AI models? Do you have the technical infrastructure to support AI deployment? Do you have the right skills and expertise in your team?

4.1.4   Identifying Use Cases

Identifying the right use cases for Generative AI is a critical part of your strategy. This involves finding the sweet spot where your business needs, AI capabilities, and data availability intersect. It could be using AI to generate content for marketing, to design new products, to automate customer service, or to make strategic decisions.

4.1.5   Developing an Implementation Plan

Your Generative AI strategy should include a detailed implementation plan. This involves deciding how to build your AI capabilities (build vs. buy), how to manage your AI projects (agile vs. waterfall), how to mitigate risks (security, bias, regulation), and how to measure success (KPIs, benchmarks).

Our work with Generative AI at SparkCognition

SparkCognition is a global leader in artificial intelligence (AI) software solutions perfected for business. In 2023, SparkCognition launched its groundbreaking Generative AI Platform, a first-of-a-kind capability focused on the needs of the industrial sector. This next-generation capability will enable organizations to apply AI even when data sets are sparse, enhancing and accelerating outcomes.

SparkCognition's Generative AI Platform for Industrials enables organizations to augment sensors and generate insights faster, with a fraction of the data at a significantly lower cost. SparkCognition's Generative AI can autonomously augment data sets by generating high-quality content in the form of synthetic text, images, audio, and other signals. As a result, customers can apply AI to problems where they couldn't previously. The SC Generative AI Platform enables a more comprehensive view of asset performance or an entire end-to-end process by enhancing low-fidelity data to provide high-fidelity insights and extrapolating low-resolution images to high-resolution views. It can also create imagery for use in simulated real-world environments, allowing organizations to analyze complex scenarios. These capabilities enable organizations to reduce the amount of foundational information needed to make informed decisions by a factor of 20X or more while executing in a fraction of the time.

To further enhance the value of its Generative AI Platform, SparkCognition is developing industry-specific large language models (LLMs)—deep learning algorithms that can recognize, summarize, translate, predict, and generate content from large unstructured datasets. The applications of this technology have broad implications on how organizations prioritize R&D investments, manage production, optimize supply, direct distribution, and more.

One of the ways we are using Generative AI at SparkCognition is to help our customers improve their maintenance practices. By generating synthetic data, we can create realistic simulations of equipment failures. This allows our customers to test and evaluate different maintenance strategies without having to risk costly downtime or damage to their equipment. We are also using Generative AI to help our customers improve their labor productivity. By generating realistic simulations of work environments, we can help our customers identify and address potential bottlenecks in their production processes. This can lead to significant improvements in efficiency and output.

Finally, we are using Generative AI to help our customers improve their business decision making. By generating realistic simulations of market conditions, we can help our customers make more informed decisions about pricing, inventory, and other key factors. This can lead to increased profits and market share.

We believe that Generative AI has the potential to revolutionize the way organizations operate. By providing organizations with the ability to generate synthetic data, we can help them to make better decisions, improve their operations, and achieve their goals.

4.1.6 Aligning with Ethics and Regulations

A responsible Generative AI strategy aligns with ethical

principles and regulatory requirements. This involves ensuring AI systems are transparent, fair, secure, and beneficial for society, and that they comply with relevant AI regulations. It also involves engaging with stakeholders to understand their expectations and concerns about AI.

4.1.7 Building Organizational Readiness

Finally, a Generative AI strategy should consider how to build organizational readiness for AI. This involves creating a culture that embraces AI, providing training and resources for employees, and establishing structures and processes to manage AI in organizations.

Developing a Generative AI strategy can be a complex and challenging process, but it is a crucial step for organizations that want to harness the power of Generative AI. With the right approach, leaders can guide their organizations to a future where Generative AI drives innovation, growth, and success.

4.2 Build a Team with the Right Skills

Creating a Generative AI initiative requires a multidisciplinary team with a diverse set of skills. This task is non-trivial, but a good place to start is to list the necessary team member roles and their corresponding competencies. This section explores the key roles that are generally needed and the skills they should possess to make the implementation of Generative AI a success.

Companies can hire these people or can partner with others to obtain these skills. An important point of awareness for leaders is to ask the following types of questions to their organization:

- Can we afford to hire for all these roles?

- Can we compete with top-tier software and AI firms to retain these individuals?

- Is the work we provide diverse and engaging enough to interest these individuals? Or are we focused on narrow problems that most leading engineers will quickly lose interest in?

- Do we have a software-first mindset in our company, or will these expensive hires become frustrated because they are constrained by what they can do and who they can interact with?

- Given the answers to all these questions, are we better off hiring and investing to build an AI company within our company, or are we better off partnering?

4.2.1 Data Scientists

Data scientists are at the forefront of any AI team. They bring expertise in machine learning algorithms and statistical models, as well as the ability to manipulate large datasets. For Generative AI, they should have a deep understanding of the latest techniques, such as GANs, VAEs, and Transformer models. They also need a knack for problem solving, to navigate the fast-evolving world of AI model building.

4.2.2 AI Engineers

AI engineers play an essential role in translating the models built by data scientists into scalable and reliable software. They are responsible for the architecture and implementation of AI systems. Their skills include programming, software engineering, cloud computing, and machine learning platforms. Knowledge of AI ethics and regulation is also a key competency.

4.2.3 Data Engineers

Data engineers are responsible for managing and preparing data for AI models. They design, build, and maintain the organization's data architecture. Skills required include database management, data cleaning, data privacy, and the ability to work with big data technologies.

4.2.4 Business Analysts

Business analysts bridge the gap between the AI team and the rest of the organization. They understand the business context, identify use cases for AI, and translate business requirements into technical specifications. Their skills include business acumen, analytical thinking, and excellent communication.

4.2.5 Product Managers

Product managers guide the development of AI products and services. They define the product vision, manage the product lifecycle, and ensure that the product meets the needs of customers and stakeholders. They need a mix of technical understanding, market insight, and leadership skills.

4.2.6   UX Designers

UX designers ensure that AI systems are user-friendly and provide a positive user experience. They design the interface, interaction, and flow of AI applications. They need skills in design thinking, user research, and interaction design.

4.2.7   Ethicists

Ethicists provide guidance on ethical issues related to AI. They help to design AI systems that are fair, transparent, and beneficial for society. They need a background in ethics, law, or social sciences, and an understanding of AI technology.

4.2.8   AI Trainers

AI trainers are responsible for training AI models. They curate and label data, monitor the training process, and fine-tune the models. They need skills in data management, machine learning, and domain expertise.

4.2.9   AI Operations Specialists

AI operations specialists manage the deployment, monitoring, and maintenance of AI systems. They ensure that the systems are running smoothly and deliver the expected performance. Skills required include DevOps, cloud computing, and IT operations.

4.2.10   Domain Experts

In specialized domains such as Energy, Manufacturing, or Pharmaceuticals, it is important to include domain experts as part of the team. They bring the discernment and knowledge that allows results to be properly analyzed, and data quality to be readily gauged. As the project matures, the need for domain experts will likely diminish, but it is important to budget substantial time with them at the inception.

Building a team with the right skills is a critical step in adopting Generative AI in an organization. It requires careful planning, recruitment, and training. It might seem daunting at first, but with each new hire, the pieces of the puzzle start to fall into place. With the right team, a company will be well-positioned to harness the power of Generative AI and transform their organization.

4.3   Select the Right Technology

The choice of the right tools and platforms for Generative AI can be difficult, especially with the rapid evolution of technology and the diverse range of options available. However, selecting the right tools can lead to productivity, efficiency, and innovation in an organization. Here, we delve into the factors to consider and some popular options available.

4.3.1   Understanding Your Needs

The first step in selecting the right tools is to understand your organization's needs. What problems are you trying to solve? What is the scale of your data? What skills does your team have? The answers to these questions will guide your selection process.

4.3.2 Tool Selection Criteria

Several criteria should guide the selection of Generative AI tools and platforms:

- **Ease of Use:** The tool should be user-friendly and have good documentation and support. It should align with your capabilities. If you don't have a very deep and available bench of AI experts, programmers, and designers, don't try to build systems from scratch.

- **Scalability:** It should be able to handle the scale of your data and computing needs.

- **Interoperability:** The tool should work well with other software and systems in your organization.

- **Security and privacy:** The tool should have robust security features and comply with data privacy regulations.

- **Cost:** Consider the cost of the tool, including licensing fees, hardware requirements, and support costs.

4.3.3 Popular Frameworks

There are several popular frameworks for Generative AI, each with its own strengths and features:

- **TensorFlow:** Developed by Google, TensorFlow is a versatile open-source platform for machine learning. It supports a wide range of neural network architectures, including those used in Generative AI.

- **PyTorch:** Developed by Meta, PyTorch is another popular open-source machine learning platform. It is known for its flexibility and ease of use, making it a favorite among researchers.

- **Keras:** Keras is a high-level neural networks API, written in Python and capable of running on top of Google's TensorFlow, Microsoft's Cognitive Toolkit (CNTK), or the open-source platform Theano. It is user-friendly, modular, and extendable, and it supports a wide range of neural network architectures.

- **OpenAI's GPT-x models:** OpenAI has released several versions of its generative pre-trained Transformers (GPT), which are state-of-the-art for many generative tasks. The primary issue with these is that they require data to be transmitted on public networks to third-party servers. Using such cloud-hosted models is impractical for many businesses that must implement secrecy, security, or comply with stringent regulatory requirements.

- **Hugging Face's Transformers:** This library provides thousands of pre-trained models to perform tasks on texts such as classification, information extraction, and, most importantly, generation.

- **Cloud AI platforms:** Many cloud providers offer AI platforms that provide a full range of tools for machine learning, from data preparation to model training and deployment. Examples include Google Cloud AI, Amazon SageMaker, and Microsoft Azure Machine Learning.

If you have a very deep and available bench of top-tier AI talent, it might make sense to use frameworks to develop your own applications; however, this is inadvisable in almost every case. The reality is that while there are many programmers who can glue together existing models into workflows, there are very few who have the experience to train large models at scale. There are even fewer who can advance the state-of-the-art from first principles. In almost every case where leaders are looking to utilize Generative AI capabilities, the right answer is to partner with high-quality, leading companies that exist only to build enterprise-ready AI platforms.

Some of these companies include:

- **SparkCognition:** An Austin-based company with the mission to deliver world-class AI solutions that allow you to solve your most critical problems, empowering you to run a more sustainable, safer, and profitable business

- **C3:** A California-based leading Enterprise AI software provider for accelerating digital transformation

- **Palantir:** A Denver-based company which makes products for human-driven analysis of real-world data

- **DataRobot:** A Boston-based leader in Value-Driven AI offering a unique and collaborative approach to Artificial Intelligence

The other consideration, of course, is whether your partner is an expensive professional services outfit or a builder of productized applications and platforms that are easy to use and inexpensive to maintain. It is quite common to get into situations where every incremental change to functionality requires an army of expensive consultants and professional services engineers to come in and execute.

Experience shows that productizing artificial intelligence platforms is non-trivial and very, very few companies have achieved these capabilities.

An Emerging Framework: Langchain

What is Langchain?

Langchain is a Python framework that provides a high-level interface for interacting with models. It is designed to be easy to use, even for developers with no experience in Python.

How does Langchain work?

Langchain works by connecting to a model and providing it with a prompt. The prompt is a natural language description of the task that a user wants the model to perform. For example, the user could provide the prompt: "Write a blog post about the latest trends in programming." The model will then generate a response based on the prompt. The response can be in any format, such as text, code, or images.

What can you do with Langchain?

Langchain can be used to develop a wide variety of applications, including:

• Blog generators

• Code generators

- Image generators

- Chatbots

- Personal assistants

- Information consultants (question answerers)

- And much more!

How do I get started with Langchain?

To get started with Langchain, you will need to:

1. Install Langchain.
2. Choose a model to use.
3. Provide a prompt to the model.
4. Get the response from the model.

For more information, please see the Langchain documentation: https://Langchain.readthedocs.io/en/latest/

Langchain provides a host of convenient abstractions that can be used to quickly develop a variety of Generative AI applications.

For those interested in developing Generative AI applications, particularly those built around LLMs, checking out Langchain is a worthwhile thing to do.

4.3.4   Custom-Built Tools

For some organizations, off-the-shelf tools may not meet their specific needs. In such cases, custom-built tools can be an option. These tools are designed and developed specifically for the organization's needs. However, they require a significant investment in time and resources.

4.3.5 Final Thoughts on Selecting the Right Technology

Selecting the right Generative AI tools and platforms is a critical step in your AI journey. While the task may seem perplexing due to the range of options and rapid technological evolution, the right choice can lead to innovation, productivity, and efficiency. By understanding your needs, considering key selection criteria, and exploring popular tools, you can make an informed decision that aligns with your organization's strategy and goals.

4.4 A Generative AI Deployment

Let's put it all together. The below diagram shows an example of a Generative AI deployment. When designing the system, all aspects of the deployment must be taken into account, from the API Frontend to the data source, security, and, in this case, multiple LLMs.

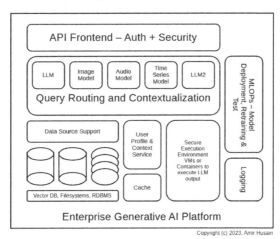

Figure 4.1: A Generative AI enterprise deployment is a complex affair with many interconnected systems, multiple LLMs and other Generative models combined with information sources, API frontends, security, logging, personalization and contextualization to name just a few integrated services.

4.5   Training Your Employees on Generative AI

The task of training employees on how to use Generative AI is a significant challenge. This process is crucial, as the most advanced technology in the world would be rendered meaningless if the workforce cannot use it effectively. Therefore, leaders must strategize and implement a comprehensive training plan that demystifies Generative AI and provides practical guidance for its application.

4.5.1   Understanding the Need for Training

Before embarking on the training journey, it is essential to comprehend the need. The realm of Generative AI, though fascinating, can be overwhelming for employees who are unfamiliar with its concepts and applications. This complexity is the first barrier to break. By providing clear, engaging training, companies can cultivate a workforce that understands and appreciates the capabilities of Generative AI and can use it to its full potential.

4.5.2   Assessing the Current Skill Level

The training strategy should start by assessing the current skill level of the employees. This allows organizations to tailor training programs to the existing knowledge base, ensuring that the training is both accessible and challenging. It is important to remember that understanding and utilizing Generative AI isn't just for technical staff. Employees across all departments, from marketing to human resources, will benefit from understanding how Generative AI can enhance their work.

71

4.5.3 Designing the Training Program

The training program should be designed with the target audience in mind. For employees with a technical background, the training might delve into the intricacies of AI algorithms, data preprocessing, and model optimization. For non-technical staff, the focus should be on understanding the applications of Generative AI, its potential benefits, and how to use AI-powered tools in their daily tasks.

4.5.4 Blending Theory and Practice

Effective training blends theory with practice. While it is important to understand the principles behind Generative AI, employees also need hands-on experience to consolidate their learning. This could involve using AI-powered tools, participating in AI projects, or working alongside AI experts. The goal is to create an environment where employees feel confident to experiment with Generative AI and learn from their experiences.

4.5.5 Ongoing Training and Support

Training shouldn't be a one-off event. As Generative AI continues to evolve, so too should the training programs. Regular updates and refresher courses can help employees stay abreast of the latest advancements and ensure they're using the technology effectively. Furthermore, creating a culture of ongoing learning can inspire employees to explore the many possibilities of AI in their own time and, in turn, bring new ideas to the organization.

4.5.6 Evaluating the Training Program

Finally, it is important to evaluate the effectiveness of the training program. This could involve testing employees' understanding of Generative AI, assessing their ability to use AI-powered tools, or soliciting their feedback on the training process. These evaluations can provide valuable insights to refine the training program and ensure it meets the needs of the workforce.

4.5.7 Final Thoughts on Training

Training employees on how to use Generative AI is a challenge that leaders must address head-on. By understanding the need for training, assessing the current skill level, designing a tailored training program, and providing ongoing support, companies can empower their workforce to harness the power of Generative AI. This, in turn, can lead to increased productivity, improved decision making, and new opportunities for growth.

4.6 Chapter Summary

- A robust Generative AI strategy begins with understanding your business context, assessing strengths, weaknesses, opportunities, and threats (SWOT), and identifying areas where Generative AI can add value.

- Your AI strategy should be guided by clear vision and goals, aligning with your overall business strategy and objectives.

- Conduct an honest assessment of your current AI capabilities, evaluating your data infrastructure, technological resources, and human capabilities.

- Identify the right use cases for Generative AI where business needs, AI capabilities, and data availability intersect.

- Your strategy should include a detailed implementation plan, considering how to build your AI capabilities, manage AI projects, mitigate risks, and measure success.

- Ensure your AI strategy aligns with ethical principles and regulatory requirements, and consider stakeholder expectations and concerns about AI.

- Building organizational readiness for AI involves creating a culture that embraces AI, providing training and resources for your employees, and establishing structures and processes to manage AI.

- Building a multidisciplinary team with a diverse set of skills is crucial for successful Generative AI implementation.

This includes data scientists, AI engineers, data engineers, business analysts, product managers, UX designers, ethicists, AI trainers, and AI operations specialists.

- The choice of tools and platforms for Generative AI should be based on your organization's needs, considering ease of use, scalability, interoperability, security, privacy, and cost.

4.7 Key Questions

1. What are the key elements to consider when formulating a Generative AI strategy for your organization?

2. How does understanding your business context influence your Generative AI strategy?

3. Why is it important to align your Generative AI strategy with your overall business strategy and objectives?

4. What are the key roles needed in a team for successful implementation of Generative AI? What skills should these individuals possess?

5. How can you identify suitable use cases for Generative AI in your organization?

6. How does aligning your AI strategy with ethical principles and regulatory requirements impact its implementation and acceptance?

7. Why is building organizational readiness for AI important, and how can you achieve it?

8. What are the key criteria to consider when selecting tools and platforms for Generative AI?

9. How does the choice of AI tools and platforms impact productivity, efficiency, and innovation in your organization?

10. What are the potential challenges when developing an AI strategy and how can they be mitigated?

Figure 4.2: ChatGPT isn't the only game in town. China's iFlyTek has launched its own "Spark" LLM-based chat service.

Figure 4.3: The Type 20 concept car from VW showcases generatively designed wheels. Photo Credit: Volkswagen

Figure 4.4: A generative furniture design, Samba, created by Guto Requena. Picture credit: Wikipedia

Figure 4.5: Volkswagen's side mirror design featuring generative structures. Photo Credit: Volkswagen

Figure 4.6: Generative Art by Refik Anadol featured at SparkCognition's Time Machine conference in Austin, Texas.

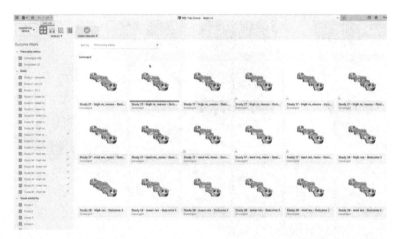

Figure 4.7: Autodesk software demonstrating the ability to create large numbers of machine-designed part variations, the best of which can be selected by the user. Photo Credit: Autodesk

Figure 4.8: Fishing pliers designed by Danco which use generative structures in the handle. Photo credit: Danco

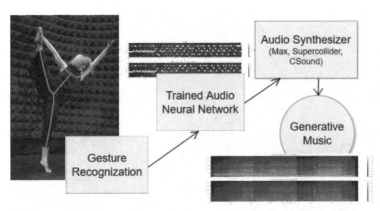

Figure 4.9: Scholars from Stony Brook University recently published a paper titled "Creating Music Through Spatial Gestures." The system can watch human interactions and use Generative AI to create musical pieces. Photo credit: Danco

Figure 4.10: The cover of author Amir Husain's book on Generative Art was designed with a generative algorithm.

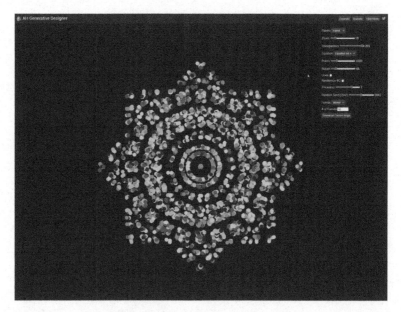

Figure 4.11: The web interface of AH Generative Designer. Modifying a few variables is all it takes to create interesting Generative Art. Source: http://openworks.cc/gd

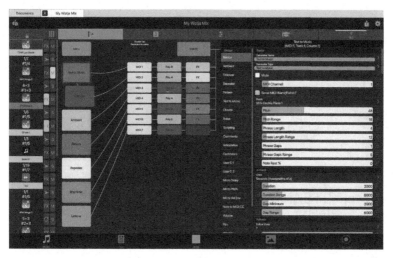

Figure 4.12: Generative music apps are exploding. This is the interface of Wotja, an innovative "Creator Player Lab" for creating generative music. It even has a Text-to-Music feature.

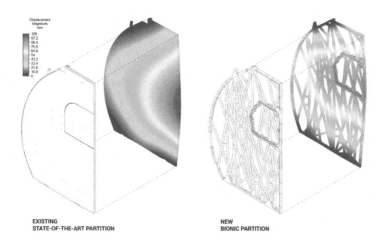

EXISTING
STATE-OF-THE-ART PARTITION

NEW
BIONIC PARTITION

Figure 4.13: Airbus used generative techniques to design a lightweight, high-strength cabin partition. The lower weight can lead to CO_2 emission reductions of up to 465,000 metric tons annually. Photo Credit: Airbus Industries

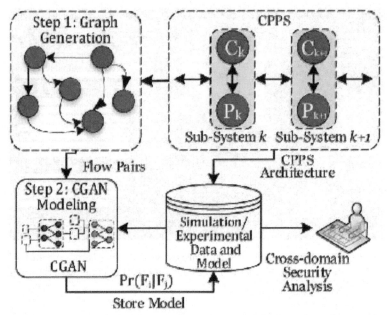

Figure 4.14: Generative Adversarial Networks will play a significant role in Cyber Security. Here is an architecture for security modeling for the analysis of Cyber-Physical systems in manufacturing. Photo credit: Sujit Rokka Chhetri, A. Lopez, and M. A. Faruque

Figure 4.15: At the Sustainable Aerospace Together Forum, Boeing's Todd Citron outlined how manufacturers are using Generative AI models to optimize aircraft design such as these futuristic concepts. Photo Credit: NASA

Chapter 5

Diving Deeper into Generative AI

5.1 Sequence Prediction Capabilities

At its core, Generative AI is about predicting and generating sequences, whether they be sequences of words, notes, or even images. Let's explore this further.

5.1.1 The Basics of Sequence Prediction

The crux of sequence prediction lies in the ability of Generative AI to take a sequence of inputs and predict what comes next. This could be the next word in a sentence, the next note in a musical composition, or even the next frame in a video. This capability is the fundamental driving force behind many of the applications of Generative AI, from text generation to music composition, image generation, and beyond.

5.1.2 Sequence Prediction in Generative AI

Sequence prediction capabilities allow Generative AI to model complex relationships within data and use these relationships to generate new, original sequences. This is the foundation of Generative AI's power and versatility. It is what allows a language model to write a paragraph, a music model to compose a symphony, or an image model to create a new piece of art.

CASE STUDY: My work with Generative Art

Generative Art is a captivating form of artistic expression that leverages algorithms, mathematics, and technology to create stunning visuals, novel effects, and deep experiences. These artistic works are not merely the product of human imagination, but the result of a collaborative process between the artist and the machine.

I, personally, have been fascinated with generative applications for a long time. Computers can so easily iterate over numerous possibilities and find beautiful pictures, interesting solutions, and novel structures that would take humans a very long time to chance upon.

Generative Art using computers has been produced for many years now. Fractals, for example, were incredibly popular in the 1980s and '90s, and a large number of programs for generating the Mandelbrot and Julia sets proliferated on home computers. In addition, genre-creating bands like Kraftwerk used simple, repetitive waveforms generated with electronics, overlayed to produce electronic music, the likes of which hadn't been heard before.

Most of the time, however, these programs were not particularly easy for non-technical users to employ. So, the interest in Generative Art remained niche, shared mainly by some artistically inclined programmers and technically inclined artists. A small universe!

AH Generative Designer

To bring knowledge of Generative Art to a wider audience and enable almost anyone to experiment with it, I wrote a book and a software program called "AH Generative Designer." This is a small but highly customizable Generative Art program designed to offer an effective introduction to the world of computational art for artists and enthusiasts. If you are not a programmer or are not comfortable modifying code to create art, you can simply use Generative Designer by manipulating its easy-to-use interface for creating mesmerizing images.

Generative Designer is written in JavaScript and uses the p5.js library. It is designed to run in a web browser and can be used on any platform that supports JavaScript. It exposes a wide range of parameters that can be customized to control the appearance of the generated images via an easy-to-use interface that allows fast experimentation with different Generative Art designs.

My book on Generative Art

I have also written a book on using computers to create art, called *Generative Art*. The draft of this book is freely available online, and it provides an introduction to the principles of Generative Art. It covers a variety of topics, including the history of Generative Art, the different types of Generative Art, the tools and techniques used to create Generative Art, the creative process of Generative Art, and the future of Generative Art.

If you get a chance to read the book and try the application, I hope you find them to be useful and inspiring!

5.1.3 Sequence Prediction Techniques

Different models use different techniques for sequence prediction. Recurrent Neural Networks (RNNs) use loops to remember previous information, which influence their predictions. However, they struggle with long sequences due to the problem of vanishing gradients.

Long Short-Term Memory (LSTM) units, a type of RNN, overcome this problem with a sophisticated mechanism that allows them to remember or forget information over longer sequences. They are widely used in tasks like language translation and speech recognition.

Transformer models, like the GPT family, leverage self-attention mechanisms to weigh the importance of different elements in a sequence when making predictions. They have proven very effective, particularly in natural language processing tasks, outperforming RNNs and LSTMs on many benchmarks.

5.1.4 Applications of Sequence Prediction

Sequence prediction capabilities open up a myriad of applications. In the realm of text, they power everything from auto-complete features in search engines to chatbots and language translation services. In music, they can be used to generate new compositions or predict the continuation of a melody. In the visual arts, they can generate new images or even predict the next frames in a video sequence. In the business world, they can forecast trends, predict customer behavior, and much more.

5.1.5 Challenges of Sequence Prediction

Despite its power, sequence prediction is not without its challenges. Models may struggle with long sequences, lose track of long-term dependencies, or generate incoherent or irrelevant outputs. There are also ethical considerations around the use of Generative AI and its potential to create misleading or harmful content.

5.1.6 The Future of Sequence Prediction

As technology advances, so too will the capabilities of sequence prediction models. Already, newer models like Transformers have shown superior performance on many tasks, and research continues to push the boundaries of what is possible. As these models become more powerful and nuanced, the applications and impact of Generative AI will only continue to grow.

5.1.7 Final Thoughts on Sequence Predictions

Sequence prediction capabilities are at the heart of Generative AI, driving its ability to create everything from text to music to images. By understanding these capabilities, leaders can better grasp the potential of Generative AI and how it can be harnessed to drive innovation and growth in their organizations. Despite the challenges and ethical considerations, the future of sequence prediction, and indeed Generative AI as a whole, is bright and full of potential.

5.2 Why Word Embeddings Are Surprisingly Effective

Word Embeddings are foundational to natural language processing (NLP) and Generative AI. They facilitate the conversion of text into numerical vectors that machines can understand and analyze. Think of a vector as an address in multi-dimensional space, just like x,y coordinates are an address in a two-dimensional space. [x,y] can be thought of as a two-dimensional vector. Now imagine vectors with a hundred scalar quantities. They would specify a point in 100-dimensional space. These spaces are impossible for humans to imagine. We live in a rather limited three-dimensional space. But computers and AI algorithms are not constrained by our human limitations. They can deal with very high dimensionality. This section of the book will delve into the concept of Word Embeddings and shed light on their effectiveness in Generative AI.

5.2.1 The Word Embedding Concept

The essence of Word Embeddings lies in their ability to encode words into multi-dimensional vectors that capture semantic relationships. The embeddings reflect the axiom that words appearing in similar contexts possess similar meanings—a concept referred to as the distributional hypothesis. Word Embeddings, such as word2Vec, GloVe, and FastText, are trained on large amounts of text data and learn to position words in high-dimensional space such that semantically similar words are closer to each other.

5.2.2   Semantic and Syntactic Relationships

One reason behind the surprising effectiveness of Word Embeddings is their capability to capture both semantic and syntactic relationships. For instance, word vectors can encode semantic relationships like "man is to woman as king is to queen," and syntactic relationships like "walking is to walked as swimming is to swam." These relationships are incredibly valuable in NLP tasks like text classification, sentiment analysis, and machine translation, making Word Embeddings a powerful tool in the Generative AI toolkit.

5.2.3   Reducing Dimensionality

High-dimensional data can be challenging to manage and process. Word Embeddings tackle this issue by reducing the dimensionality of text data. They map each word to a fixed-length vector, regardless of the size of the vocabulary. This dimensionality reduction not only makes the data more manageable but also helps in revealing patterns and relationships that might be obscured in the high-dimensional space.

5.2.4   Handling Out-of-Vocabulary Words

Traditional one-hot encoding methods struggle to handle words not present in the training data. However, certain Word Embedding techniques like FastText can generate embeddings for out-of-vocabulary words by breaking down words into sub-word units, such as character n-grams. This feature adds a layer of robustness to NLP models, allowing them to handle unfamiliar words and languages with rich morphology.

5.2.5   Transfer Learning and Domain Adaptability

Word Embeddings facilitate transfer learning, wherein a model trained on one task can be applied to another task. Pre-trained Word Embeddings can be used as the starting point for various NLP tasks, reducing the need for extensive training data and computational resources. Moreover, Word Embeddings can be fine-tuned to adapt to specific domains, enhancing their effectiveness in specialized contexts.

5.2.6   Contextualized Word Embeddings

The latest advancements in Word Embeddings, such as ELMo, BERT, and GPT, generate contextualized embeddings. Unlike traditional Word Embeddings that assign the same vector to a word regardless of its context, these models generate different vectors for a word based on its surrounding words. This ability to capture context-specific meanings has led to significant improvements in various NLP tasks, further underlining the effectiveness of Word Embeddings.

5.2.7   Final Thoughts on Word Embeddings

Word Embeddings may initially confuse newcomers to the field of Generative AI, but their effectiveness is surprisingly evident once understood. By encoding semantic and syntactic relationships, reducing dimensionality, handling out-of-vocabulary words, facilitating transfer learning, and capturing context-specific meanings, Word Embeddings have revolutionized NLP and Generative AI. As we continue to refine and develop these techniques, we can anticipate even more sophisticated and nuanced applications of Generative AI, with Word Embeddings as their cornerstone.

5.3 Large Language Models LLMs

Large Language Models (LLMs) like GPT-3 and BERT have revolutionized the field of natural language processing (NLP). Their complexity and effectiveness have made them a pivotal topic for understanding Generative AI. This section will demystify LLMs and explain their role in the field.

5.3.1 Understanding LLMs

At their core, LLMs are neural network-based models designed to understand, generate, and manipulate human language. They are "large" due to the vast number of parameters they contain, often reaching into the billions. These parameters enable LLMs to learn from and generate complex, nuanced textual data, making them capable of remarkable tasks such as language translation, text summarization, and even creative writing.

5.3.2 Training LLMs

LLMs are trained on vast amounts of text data. They learn to predict the next word in a sentence given the preceding words, a process known as autoregressive language modelling. This mechanism allows LLMs to understand grammar, context, and even cultural references, metaphors, and idioms. The models are unsupervised, which means they learn directly from raw text data without needing explicit labels.

5.3.3 Capabilities of LLMs

The capabilities of LLMs are diverse and continually expanding. They can generate human-like text, answer complex questions, write code, and even create poetry or prose. They can understand sentiment, extract information, and summarize long documents. These capabilities have made LLMs invaluable across many industries, from customer service and content creation to healthcare and law.

5.3.4 Fine-Tuning LLMs

As we mentioned, LLMs have proven their value as versatile tools in a variety of applications. From generating human-like text to answering complex queries, these models, when properly trained, can perform impressive feats of AI prowess. However, their real power becomes evident when they are fine-tuned for specific tasks, industries, or companies. Fine-tuning an LLM involves taking the foundational model—which has been pre-trained on a broad corpus of data—and further training it on a specialized dataset relevant to the task at hand. This might be data from a particular field like medical literature for healthcare applications, or corporate documents for business applications. Fine-tuning effectively extends the model's knowledge, making it more accurate and useful in the specific context in which it will be used.

5.3.5 The Art of Prompt Engineering

Despite their power, LLMs are not yet mind-readers. Extracting useful information from them requires skill and experience, a practice known as prompt engineering. This involves providing the LLM with context or cues—the prompts—that help it generate the desired output.

The art of prompt engineering lies in understanding how the model "thinks" and crafting prompts that guide it towards the desired outcome without leading it too strongly or leaving it too vague. This might involve experimentation, iterating, and refining prompts based on the model's responses. It is a form of dialogue between human and machine, requiring a deep understanding of both the task at hand and the workings of the model.

5.3.6 Data Leakage in Fine-Tuning and Prompt Engineering

While fine-tuning and prompt engineering can enhance the performance of LLMs, they also raise the risk of data leakage. This is when private or sensitive information, included in the training data or prompts, inadvertently makes its way into the model's outputs, potentially making it accessible to others who use the model.

For instance, if an LLM is fine-tuned on company documents that include proprietary information, the model might generate text that references or hints at this information. Similarly, prompts that contain sensitive details can lead the model to generate responses that include these details. Both cases represent data leakage, which can pose privacy and security risks.

5.3.7 Shared vs. Private LLMs

Large tech companies and cloud providers are increasingly

offering "LLM as a service," where users can access pre-trained models via the cloud. These shared models offer advantages such as convenience and minimal IT setup overhead, but raise major issues around data privacy and control.

An alternative is for a company to develop its own LLM. However, training an LLM from scratch is a daunting task requiring substantial resources. A more feasible option for many is to start with an open-source foundational model and fine-tune it on their own data. This offers a balance between control and feasibility, allowing companies to leverage the power of LLMs while maintaining control over their data and model behavior.

5.3.8 Hallucinations in LLM Outputs

While LLMs can generate remarkably human-like text, they're not perfect. One notable issue is the tendency to "hallucinate," or generate information that wasn't in their training data and isn't true. This is because LLMs are optimized for creativity and coherence, not factual accuracy.

In applications where accuracy is critical, this can be a problem. One strategy is to use LLMs in contexts where brain-storming is useful, or where outputs can be verified. This harnesses the creative power of the models while mitigating the risks of their hallucinations.

5.3.9 Transparency and Explainability

LLMs, like many neural networks, are often described as "black boxes." Their decision-making processes are hard to interpret, and their outputs can sometimes be surprising or difficult to explain. This lack of transparency and explainability is a fundamental limitation of the technology, and it raises challenges in terms of accountability, trustworthiness, and regulatory compliance.

Despite these challenges, progress is being made. Researchers are developing methods for better understanding the internal workings of these models, as well as techniques to make them more interpretable and controllable. However, these are active areas of research, and full transparency and explainability are still some way off.

It is worth noting that, while some LLM offerings may claim to offer full transparency and explainability, these claims should be viewed with caution. Given the current state of the art, such claims are often overblown and can be misleading. A thorough evaluation and understanding of the technology is necessary before any deployment. Ultimately, transparency and explainability in AI should be about building systems that operate in a way that is understandable and trustworthy to humans.

5.3.10   The Power of Transfer Learning

One of the key strengths of LLMs is their ability to leverage transfer learning. After being trained on a large corpus of text, an LLM can be fine-tuned on a specific task with a much smaller dataset. This process enables the model to adapt its vast language knowledge to specific applications, making it an efficient solution for numerous NLP tasks.

5.3.11   Understanding Context with Transformers

A major breakthrough in LLMs was the introduction of the Transformer architecture, a model structure that uses self-attention mechanisms to understand the context of each word in relation to all other words in a text. This capacity to capture both local and global context has significantly improved the performance of LLMs, enabling them to generate more coherent and contextually accurate text.

5.3.12   Handling Ambiguity

Language is often ambiguous and context-dependent, which can make it challenging for machines to understand. LLMs, however, can handle such ambiguity effectively. By considering the broader context, LLMs can disambiguate words and understand nuanced meanings, enabling them to produce more accurate and contextually appropriate outputs.

5.3.13   Challenges and Limitations of LLMs

Despite their impressive capabilities, LLMs also have their challenges. They require vast amounts of data and computational resources, which can make them inaccessible for some organizations. They can also inadvertently generate biased or harmful content if such content is present in their training data. Additionally, while LLMs can generate coherent text, they do not truly understand the text in the way humans do. They do not have beliefs, desires, or intentions, and their outputs are purely a reflection of the patterns they have learned from their training data.

5.3.14   Zero-shot, One-shot, and Few-shot Learning

LLMs like GPT-3 can perform tasks without any specific task training, a capability known as zero-shot learning. They can also learn from a single example (one-shot learning) or a few examples (few-shot learning). This flexibility makes them incredibly powerful and adaptable, as they can handle a wide range of tasks without needing extensive task-specific training data.

5.3.15   Final Thoughts on LLMs

In this bewildering world of language and learning, LLMs stand as a testament to the potential of Generative AI. Their ability to generate coherent, contextually aware text is a transformative tool that organizations can utilize for a myriad of applications, from automating customer service responses to generating engaging content.

However, it is crucial to remember that, while LLMs possess incredible language mimicry, they lack true understanding or consciousness. They generate outputs based on learned patterns, not from a place of comprehension or intent. This can lead to unexpected or inappropriate outputs if the models encounter unfamiliar or sensitive topics. Ensuring the ethical and responsible use of LLMs is a significant responsibility for leaders implementing these models in their organizations.

Moreover, the computational cost and data requirements for training LLMs are high, which may pose a barrier for some organizations. Still, the increasing availability of pre-trained models and cloud-based AI services is making

LLMs more accessible to a wider range of businesses.

Finally, it is essential to recognize the potential for bias in LLM outputs. Since LLMs learn from data, any bias in that data can be reflected in the model's outputs. Leaders must be aware of this and implement strategies to mitigate potential bias, ensuring that the use of LLMs aligns with the organization's values and commitment to fairness and inclusivity.

In the face of these challenges, the potential of LLMs remains robust. Their ability to understand and generate text, combined with their versatility and adaptability, makes them a powerful tool in the Generative AI toolkit. By understanding their capabilities and limitations, leaders can harness the power of LLMs to drive innovation and efficiency in their organizations. As we move into a future increasingly shaped by AI, understanding and utilizing tools like LLMs will become not just advantageous, but essential.

5.4   The Use of Tools with LLMs

In the world of Generative AI, tools and applications leveraging LLMs are not only becoming increasingly prevalent, they're also driving transformative change across industries. However, to harness the full power of LLMs, it is essential to understand how to effectively integrate them into existing systems and workflows. The selection, adoption, and strategic use of the right tools can empower organizations, enhancing efficiency, innovation, and competitiveness.

LLMs are powerful tools that can be used for a variety of tasks, including generating text, translating languages, writing different kinds of creative content, and answering questions in an informative way. However, LLMs are not limited to these tasks. They can also be used in conjunction with other tools to perform even more complex tasks.

One way to use tools with LLMs is to add extensions to the LLM's workflow. Extensions are small programs that can be added to an LLM to give it new capabilities. For example, an extension could be used to allow the LLM to access external information, such as the weather forecast or stock prices. Extensions can also be used to improve the LLM's performance on specific tasks, such as translation or writing.

Another way to use tools with LLMs is to integrate them with other software applications. For example, an LLM could be integrated with a word processing application to allow users to generate text directly in the document. Or, an LLM could be integrated with a customer relationship management (CRM) system to allow users to generate personalized marketing materials.

The use of tools with LLMs is still in its early stages, but it has the potential to revolutionize the way we interact with computers. By combining the power of LLMs with the capabilities of other tools, we can create new and powerful applications that can help us to be more productive, creative, and informed.

Here are some examples of how tools are being used with LLMs today:

- Google Translate uses LLMs to improve the accuracy of its translations.

- Grammarly uses LLMs to help users improve their grammar and spelling.

- QuillBot uses LLMs to help users rewrite their text more effectively.

- ProWritingAid uses LLMs to help users identify and correct errors in their writing.

- Writesonic uses LLMs to help users generate content, such as articles, blog posts, and social media posts.

- Hugging Face provides a platform for developers to build and share LLM models.

- OpenAI provides a suite of tools for developers to use with LLMs.

These are just a few examples of how tools are being used with LLMs today. As LLMs continue to develop, we can expect to see even more innovative and powerful applications that use this technology.

The use of tools with LLMs is a promising area of research with the potential to revolutionize the way we interact with computers. By combining the power of LLMs with the capabilities of other tools, we can create new and powerful applications that can help us to be more productive, creative, and informed.

In addition to the examples listed above, there are many other ways that tools can be used with LLMs. For example, LLMs can be used to:

- Generate creative content such as poems, stories, and scripts

- Translate languages in real time

- Write different kinds of technical documentation

- Answer questions in an informative way, even if they are open-ended, challenging, or strange

- Help users learn new things by generating summaries of factual topics

The possibilities are endless! As LLMs continue to develop, we can expect to see even more innovative and powerful applications that use this technology.

Despite the promise of these tools, it is important to approach them with a degree of informed skepticism. The outputs of an LLM are entirely dependent on the inputs it receives, the data it was trained on, and the fine-tuning it has undergone. As a result, these models can sometimes produce outputs that are inaccurate, misleading, or biased. It is crucial for leaders to understand these limitations and implement appropriate safeguards.

To effectively use LLM-powered tools, organizations should focus on a few key areas. First, invest in training teams on how to use these tools effectively. This involves understanding not just the technical aspects, but also the ethical implications and potential risks associated with their use.

Second, establish clear guidelines and policies for the use of these tools. This includes defining what constitutes acceptable use, ensuring compliance with data privacy regulations, and setting up processes for quality control and bias mitigation.

Third, create a feedback loop for continuous improvement. Monitor the performance of these tools, gather user feedback, and use these insights to improve and optimize AI strategy.

The world of Generative AI may seem daunting, and ceding control to have LLMs invoke external tools may at first appear scary. But, with the right safety frameworks in place, the potential rewards for those who navigate this shift successfully are immense. By understanding and effectively using tools powered by Large Language Models, organizations can unlock new levels of efficiency, innovation, and customer satisfaction. In the fast-evolving landscape of AI, those who learn to harness the power of these tools will be the ones leading the charge into the future.

5.5   Chapter Summary

- Generative AI is essentially about predicting and generating sequences, whether they be sequences of words, notes, or images. This capability underpins many applications of Generative AI, including text generation, music composition, and image generation.

- Sequence prediction in Generative AI models complex relationships within data to generate new, original sequences. It is the mechanism that enables a language model to write a paragraph or a music model to compose a symphony.

- Different models use different techniques for sequence prediction, including Recurrent Neural Networks (RNNs), Long Short-Term Memory (LSTM) units, and Transformer models like the GPT family.

- Sequence prediction capabilities open up various applications in text, music, visual arts, and business, including autocomplete features, chatbots, language translation, trend forecasting, and more.

- Challenges in sequence prediction include handling long sequences, maintaining long-term dependencies, generating coherent outputs, and addressing ethical considerations.

- The future of sequence prediction involves technological advancements, improvements in model capabilities, and an increased impact of Generative AI on various applications.

- Word Embeddings are foundational to natural language processing (NLP) and Generative AI, encoding words into multi-dimensional vectors that capture semantic relationships and making text data manageable for machine learning.

5.6   Key Questions

1. How do sequence prediction capabilities drive the applications of Generative AI, such as text generation, music composition, and image generation?

2. What are the different techniques used for sequence prediction, and how do they differ in terms of their advantages and disadvantages?

3. In what ways can sequence prediction capabilities be applied across various domains, including text, music, visual arts, and business?

4. What are the challenges and ethical considerations associated with sequence prediction in Generative AI?

5. How can advancements in technology and model capabilities shape the future of sequence prediction and its applications?

6. What role do Word Embeddings play in Generative AI and natural language processing, and how do they contribute to the effectiveness of these models?

7. How do contextualized Word Embeddings, such as ELMo, BERT, and GPT, improve upon traditional Word Embeddings in capturing context-specific meanings?

Chapter 6

Is Generative Content Detectable?

6.1 Introduction

This chapter is based on some of the bleeding-edge research work currently in progress to identify AI-generated content by inserting "fingerprints" or identifiable markers in the content. My wife, Zaib, and I supported the establishment of The University of Texas at Austin's Institute for Machine Learning (IFML) with an inaugural grant, which was followed by the National Science Foundation with additional funding. As a consequence, the IFML was established as a leading global center for Machine Learning research.

In April 2023, Professor Scott Aaronson of UT Austin spoke at the Amir & Zaib Husain Auditorium on methods he is investigating to help detect content produced by Generative AI technologies. This chapter is based on Scott's talk.

6.2 Understanding AI and the Motivation for Watermarking

The sudden surge of OpenAI's GPT-3, though not an enormous technological leap over the previously available models, became a profound catalyst for discussions about understanding and monitoring the outputs of AI models. A critical focus has been on the creation of a tool for statistical watermarking of GPT outputs, a significant stride towards identifying AI-generated content.

AI systems are becoming increasingly powerful and complex, yet our understanding of why and how they generate particular outputs remains limited. This scenario presents a problem, especially when it comes to aligning AI with human values. This led to the exploration of neural cryptography, a field aimed at implementing cryptographic functionality in AI systems. The goal of watermarking, a core aspect of neural cryptography, is to insert a statistical signal into a GPT's output, making it possible to trace the origin of the content. This concept addresses the potential misuse of AI, ranging from academic cheating to propaganda, spam, and impersonation.

6.3   Comparisons with Other Methods of Detection

While watermarking presents a potential solution, it is not the only approach for distinguishing AI-generated text from human text. There are also discriminator models that have been trained to do this, such as GPT Zero and OpenAI's detect GPT. However, these models are far from perfect. Furthermore, GPT's purpose is to emulate human-like text generation, which inherently challenges these models. Another alternative is storing all generated outputs in a database for later reference, but this raises serious privacy concerns.

6.4   The Mechanics of Watermarking

Watermarking works by utilizing a pseudo-random function. GPT generates a probability distribution over the next token, which usually leads to a variety of outputs. By manipulating this process through the pseudo-random function, the output can be made to favor tokens that result in a higher water-marking score. This systematic bias changes the mean score in watermarked text, making it distinguishable from text that is not watermarked. The effectiveness of this method is dependent on the entropy of the text, with higher entropy allowing for more watermarking.

6.5   Challenges and Countermeasures

Despite its promise, the watermarking method isn't flawless. Simple modifications, such as translating the text to a different language or inserting and then removing specific words, can effectively obliterate the watermark. The method is robust against local modifications but struggles with global changes. Potential countermeasures include applying filters for evasion attempts and watermarking at smaller engrams, but a more conceptual watermarking method remains a challenging research question.

6.6   Further Developments and Thoughts

Other explorations in this field involve inserting a cryptographic backdoor into a machine learning model, which presents its own set of challenges and opportunities. The study also extends to the theory of acceleration risk, which is trying to determine when to halt the scaling of machine learning models to prevent unforeseen risks.

The quest to detect AI-generated content is a multifaceted problem with a combination of potential solutions. The development of neural cryptography, particularly watermarking, is a promising approach to the problem, but it is not without its challenges. As AI continues to evolve, so too must our methods for understanding, aligning, and monitoring it.

6.7   Chapter Summary

- Cutting-edge research to identify AI-generated content is investigating inserting unique identifiers or "finger-prints" into machine created content.

- The motivation for watermarking is driven in large part by the surge of OpenAI's GPT-3 and the challenges in understanding and controlling AI outputs.

- Watermarking is a part of neural cryptography, aiming to insert a statistical signal into a GPT's output to trace the content's origin and prevent misuse of AI.

- Other methods of distinguishing AI-generated content, like discriminator models and storing all generated outputs, have significant limitations.

- The mechanics of watermarking involve a pseudo-random function to manipulate the token generation process, thus causing a systematic bias in the output.

- Despite its potential, watermarking faces challenges, as modifications like translating the text or adding and removing specific words can remove the watermark.

- Further developments in this field include inserting a cryptographic backdoor into a machine learning model and exploring the theory of acceleration risk.

- The development of neural cryptography, particularly watermarking, is a promising approach to identifying AI-generated content, but it is not without its challenges.

6.8   Key Questions

1. What is the motivation behind the development of water-marking techniques for AI-generated content?

2. How does watermarking work, and what role does the pseudo-random function play in this process?

3. What are the limitations of other methods of identifying AI-generated content, such as discriminator models and output databases?

4. What challenges does the watermarking method face, and what potential countermeasures are being considered?

5. What are some of the further developments and explorations in the field of neural cryptography, and how might they contribute to the detection of AI-generated content?

6. How does the theory of acceleration risk relate to the scaling of machine learning models, and why is this an important consideration?

7. Given the challenges and limitations of current methods, what might be future directions for improving our ability to identify and control AI-generated content?

Chapter 7

A Generative AI Future

7.1   The Impact of Generative AI on Society

As Generative AI continues to evolve and permeate different aspects of life, its impact on society is a topic of fervent discussion. The potential implications are vast, complex, and at times ambiguous, reflecting the dual-edged nature of this transformative technology.

On one hand, Generative AI holds the promise of catalyzing unprecedented advancements. It can enhance productivity and efficiency across industries, from automating mundane tasks to enabling rapid innovation. In healthcare, it could streamline diagnostics and treatment planning, while in education, personalized learning experiences could be created for each student. In the realm of content creation, it could democratize access to high-quality material, enabling creators to produce compelling content with ease.

Furthermore, the applications of Generative AI could provide solutions to some of society's most pressing issues. For instance, in the face of climate change, Generative AI models could be used to predict weather patterns and assist in designing more efficient renewable energy systems. In the fight against misinformation, AI could assist in identifying and flagging fake news or manipulated media.

However, the very capabilities that make Generative AI so promising also open the door to potential misuse and unintended consequences. As we ride the crest of this wave of AI-driven innovation, we also need to grapple with its implications—the sudden and unpredictable societal impact that could catch us off guard.

In the realm of privacy and security, the ability of Generative AI to create realistic synthetic content raises concerns. Deepfakes, or AI-generated images, videos, and audio, can be used to fabricate convincing but false narratives, contributing to the spread of misinformation and posing significant risks to personal privacy and public trust.

Bias is another critical concern. As Generative AI models learn from existing data, they can inadvertently perpetuate and amplify existing biases. This can lead to unfair outcomes in decision-making applications, from hiring and lending to law enforcement and healthcare.

The automation potential of Generative AI also raises questions about job displacement. While it can free up human time for more complex and creative tasks, it could also render certain roles obsolete, leading to job loss and exacerbating social inequality.

Moreover, the unprecedented power and complexity of Generative AI systems present challenges in terms of accountability and transparency. Traditional methods of oversight and regulation may not suffice in the face of AI systems that can generate outputs autonomously and whose decision-making processes are not easily interpretable by humans.

As we stand at this crossroads, it is clear that the path ahead is filled with both immense promise and formidable challenges. The key to navigating this future is approaching it with a sense of shared responsibility.

Regulators, technologists, and society at large must engage in open and informed dialogues to understand the potential impacts of Generative AI on society. Leaders in particular have a critical role to play in guiding this conversation, advocating for policies and practices that ensure the benefits of Generative AI are widely shared while its risks are thoughtfully mitigated.

Ultimately, the future of Generative AI and its impacts on society will be shaped by the choices we make today. By embracing the potential of this technology, while staying vigilant to its challenges, we can ensure that the future of Generative AI is one that benefits all of society.

Future Cities: How NEOM might use Generative AI

The city of NEOM in Saudi Arabia represents a futuristic vision of urban life, extensively integrating AI and other advanced technologies. Here are the key takeaways from an interview with one of the designers:

- **Cognitive Community:** NEOM aims to create the world's first cognitive community, with a technology ecosystem that's intuitive, predictive, and immersive. This is accomplished through advanced computing systems, a diverse partner network, and a strong emphasis on differential privacy.

- **Seamless Society:** NEOM envisions a society where technology creates an interconnected, intelligent, and resilient environment. It aims to provide a predictive, personalized, and immersive experience, enabled by autonomous, self-healing services that enhance daily life. In this society, individuals can collaborate without barriers, with a system that values and nurtures their uniqueness.

- **Next-Generation AI:** This ambitious project requires ingenuity and leading-edge problem solving. The result will be a user experience that feels intuitive and predictive, simplifying and enhancing life.

- **Advanced Robotics:** NEOM is exploring the use of robotics to bring speed, strength, accuracy, and precision to various tasks. The city aims to develop new solutions that foster real synergy in the human-machine relationship, paving the way for a future of trust and true collaboration.

- **Cognitive Ecosystem:** By building a cognitive technology infrastructure, NEOM creates opportunities for businesses to leverage connectivity, computing capacity, predictive analytics, and immersive capabilities. This ecosystem encourages innovation, job creation, and continuous development.

- **Trust and Data Privacy:** NEOM emphasizes that trust is crucial for a cognitive experience. It aims to empower its citizens to control their data privacy and embrace this new way of living at their own pace. As trust is built, more personalized, predictive, and autonomous services can be offered.

NEOM's innovative blueprint for technology-enhanced living might inspire other nations and cities to explore similar initiatives.

Let's analyze use cases for Generative AI given the goals for NEOM we've summarized previously.

First, NEOM is likely to require thousands of robotics use cases. Training robots on physical, real-world data will be expensive and costly. Generative AI can be used to create virtual environments and use them to generate synthetic data for training.

Second, the city will have massive displays and digital experiences. In order to deliver frequently updated, engaging content, city officials might consider using Generative AI to automatically create imagery, animations, soundscapes, and video to essentially have access to a relatively low-cost, constantly refreshing, and novel source of data.

Third, the city will be overflowing with sensors. The number of needed sensors can be reduced by enhancing the accuracy and sensitivity of each sensor, using Generative techniques like those covered earlier in this book while discussing the Shell and SparkCognition collaboration on seismic imagery.

These are just a few of the ways in which Generative AI can be used to enable and invigorate the NEOM vision. The technology most definitely has tremendous potential to be applied to future smart cities.

7.2   Will Generative AI be Used for Good?

Ensuring the responsible use of Generative AI is a daunting

task, one that demands a multifaceted approach. It requires the concerted effort of multiple stakeholders: technologists, policymakers, business leaders, and society at large.

To begin, there's a crucial role for developers and researchers in designing and training AI models responsibly. This involves considering ethics at every stage of the development process. It means carefully curating and vetting training data to mitigate the risk of bias. It also means developing robust methods to detect and filter out inappropriate or harmful content generated by AI models. Furthermore, researchers should strive to make their models as transparent and interpretable as possible, to allow for scrutiny and accountability.

Next, organizations that deploy Generative AI must exercise due diligence. They need to establish clear guidelines and protocols for AI use, taking into account legal, ethical, and societal implications. They should also invest in training their employees to use AI responsibly and understand both its capabilities and limitations. When AI is used to make decisions, it is important that these decisions are auditable and that there is a clear mechanism for redress in case of errors or unfair outcomes.

Policymakers, too, have a significant role to play. They need to develop a comprehensive regulatory framework for Generative AI, one that balances the need for innovation with the protection of individual rights and societal values. This includes regulations around data privacy, intellectual property, accountability, and transparency. It also includes policies to mitigate the potential negative impacts of AI, such as job displacement. Policymakers should also promote digital literacy, ensuring that citizens understand AI and can engage in informed discussions about its use.

In addition, the academic community can contribute by conducting rigorous research on the societal impacts of Generative AI. They can assess the effectiveness of different strategies for mitigating bias, evaluate the impact of AI on jobs, and explore ways to make AI systems more transparent and accountable.

Lastly, society at large plays a crucial role in shaping the use of Generative AI. Public awareness and engagement can drive demand for responsible AI practices, influencing the behavior of businesses and policymakers. Civil society organizations can advocate for the rights of individuals and communities affected by AI, while the media can play a key role in scrutinizing AI use and raising awareness of its implications.

Ensuring that Generative AI is used for good is an ongoing, dynamic process, not a one-time task. It requires continual monitoring and adjustment, as technology evolves and as we learn more about its impacts. It also requires an open and inclusive dialogue, where diverse perspectives are heard and valued.

This task may seem daunting, given the complexity and rapid pace of AI development. However, the stakes are too high to be ignored. The choices we make today will shape the future of Generative AI and its impact on society. By approaching this challenge with foresight, responsibility, and a commitment to shared values, we can harness the power of Generative AI to create a better future for all.

7.3   AI Regulation or More Education?

In May, 2023, Sam Altman, the chief executive of OpenAI,

testified before Congress, calling for regulatory limits on powerful AI systems such as OpenAI's GPT-3. Some in the industry interpreted this as an altruistic move driven by genuine concern, while others considered it a way to kick the ladder to prevent the competition from climbing to where OpenAI has already reached. Regardless of how one sees this particular event, it is clear that the explosive arrival of Generative AI has indeed caused much anxiety about economic loss, societal disruption, and existential risks. However, while the regulatory conversation ensues, it is crucial to acknowledge and address a deeply rooted problem in our society—a widespread lack of literacy and poor standards of education that make discerning fact from fiction a challenge.

The real insurance against disinformation is the ability of citizens to sift fact from fiction through knowledge, logic, a good education, and the application of the scientific method. If the richest country in the world fails to provide its own citizens with a high-quality education, then no amount of regulation will stop Generative AI disinformation, or even human-created propaganda, from taking root.

In the United States, there is presently great interest in developing AI regulation. In Congress, Senate Majority Leader Chuck Schumer is calling for legislative "guardrails" on AI products and services. The Biden Administration is pushing the blueprint for an AI Bill of Rights. In Europe, too, there are knee-jerk reactions, such as Italy banning GPT-3.

The European Union is now developing an AI Act. US federal agencies, such as the Department of Commerce and the Federal Trade Commission, are also weighing in on the discussion, offering their perspectives on how AI systems should be audited and monitored. There is no question that the regulatory landscape is becoming more complex.

When the only tool one has is a hammer, everything looks like a nail. Regulation is certainly an important aspect of the AI conversation, but focusing solely on it could obscure a more fundamental issue—the role of education in empowering individuals to navigate the digital landscape. Lies cannot be eliminated by sewing people's lips closed or banning ink. Instead of attempting to regulate every instance of potential misinformation, it might be more effective to ensure that individuals have the tools to discern fact from fiction. This approach acknowledges that disinformation cannot be completely eradicated and instead focuses on equipping people to deal with it.

The statistics are sobering. Currently, 45 million Americans (13%) are functionally illiterate and cannot read above a fifth-grade level. Half of all adults cannot read a book written at an eighth-grade level, and 57% of students failed the California Standards Test in English. Only one-third of fourth-graders reach the proficient reading level, and just 25% of students in California school systems can perform basic reading skills. This problem extends into the adult population as well, with 85% of juvenile offenders and 60% of people in American prisons struggling with reading. Furthermore, 75% of people on welfare can't read. These statistics underline the urgent need for a more literate society, one equipped to deal with the complexities and challenges of the digital age.

In an age where AI can generate highly convincing text, the ability to critically evaluate information becomes more important than ever.

So, perhaps as our lawmakers push regulation, it is fair to ask them what they are simultaneously doing to confront the more significant issue of widespread illiteracy and lack of education.

As AI becomes more integrated into our everyday lives, it should be self-evident that the problem of disinformation cannot be solved by technology or regulation alone. Nelson Mandela once said, "Education is the most powerful weapon which you can use to change the world." As we face the challenges of disinformation and the rapid advancement of AI technology, these words ring truer today than ever before.

Focusing on regulation without addressing the underlying problem of illiteracy is like putting a band-aid on a bullet wound. Regulation can set boundaries, but it is education that empowers. To truly address the challenge of disinformation in the age of AI, we must combine regulatory measures with a renewed commitment to education. This two-pronged approach, embracing both technological advancement and human development, will pave the way for a more literate, informed, and resilient society. The most potent tool we have is the power of an enlightened mind.

7.4   Chapter Summary

- Generative AI holds the promise of unprecedented advancements across various industries, but also poses significant risks related to misuse and unintended consequences.

- Applications of Generative AI could address pressing societal issues like climate change and misinformation, but it could also contribute to these issues through the creation of deepfakes and the spread of misinformation.

- Generative AI can perpetuate and amplify existing biases, leading to unfair outcomes in various sectors, including hiring, lending, law enforcement, and health-care.

- The automation potential of Generative AI raises concerns about job displacement and social inequality.

- The complexity of Generative AI systems presents challenges in terms of accountability and transparency, as traditional methods of oversight and regulation may be inadequate.

- Regulators, technologists, and society at large must engage in open and informed dialogues to understand and miti-gate the potential impacts of Generative AI on society.

- Ensuring responsible use of Generative AI requires concerted effort from multiple stakeholders, including developers, organizations, policymakers, the academic community, and society at large.

- Developers and researchers should consider ethics at all

stages of AI development, curate training data to mitigate bias, develop methods to filter harmful content, and strive for model transparency and interpretability.

- Policymakers need to develop comprehensive regulations that balance innovation with the protection of individual rights and societal values and promote digital literacy.

- The academic community can contribute by conducting rigorous research on the societal impacts of Generative AI, while society and civil organizations can drive demand for responsible AI practices.

7.5   Key Questions

1. What are the potential positive and negative impacts of Generative AI on society across various sectors, such as healthcare, education, and content creation?

2. How can Generative AI both aid in combating societal issues like climate change and misinformation, and contribute to these issues?

3. What are the implications of Generative AI in terms of privacy, security, and the spread of bias?

4. How might the automation potential of Generative AI affect job markets and social inequality?

5. What are the challenges in terms of accountability and transparency when dealing with Generative AI systems?

6. What roles do various stakeholders, such as developers, organizations, policymakers, the academic community, and society at large, play in ensuring the responsible use of Generative AI?

7. What strategies can developers and researchers employ to mitigate the risks associated with Generative AI, such as bias and harmful content generation?

8. How can policymakers and the academic community contribute to the responsible use and regulation of Generative AI?

9. What role can society and civil organizations play in shaping the use of Generative AI and advocating for responsible AI practices?

Chapter 8

To Boldly Go...

8.1 How Can CEOs Prepare for the Future of Generative AI?

As we approach the close of our exploration into Generative AI, it is essential to circle back to the people at the helm of our organizations—the CEOs and leaders. How can they prepare for this future that is already unfolding?

Firstly, CEOs must embrace a learning mindset. Generative AI, with all its subtleties and nuances, is not a field that one can grasp fully overnight. It requires continuous learning and adaptation, an understanding that evolves and grows with the technology itself. Investing time in understanding the potential, the functionality, and the ethical implications of Generative AI will be crucial. Reading widely, attending seminars, engaging with AI experts, and perhaps most importantly, asking the right questions, will all contribute to a well-rounded understanding of this transformative technology.

Secondly, cultivating a culture of innovation and agility within the organization is paramount. The implementation of Generative AI is not a linear process. It will be marked by advancements, frustration, challenges, breakthroughs, and setbacks. Fostering an environment that is resilient to these fluctuations and encourages experimentation will ensure that the organization is not left behind.

Thirdly, it is vital for CEOs to lead with ethics and responsibility. The power of Generative AI comes with significant ethical considerations. CEOs must ensure their organization's use of AI aligns with its core values and societal norms. This involves establishing clear guidelines, promoting transparency, and advocating for fairness and inclusivity in all AI-driven processes.

Finally, CEOs must look ahead and strategically plan for a future interwoven with AI. This involves foreseeing potential impacts on the workforce, preparing for regulatory changes, and considering the implications on business models and strategies. CEOs should also identify opportunities that Generative AI could open up in the future—new markets, products, services, and ways of working that might currently be beyond our imagination.

8.2   Where to Start Now

Generative AI offers a wide range of applications across various business domains. From marketing to software engineering, mechanical engineering to cybersecurity, sales to finance, accounting to legal, Generative AI can automate tasks, personalize experiences, and enhance productivity. To get started, let's review a list of 75 tasks and processes to which organizations could immediately apply Generative AI. These tasks do not require new technology to be developed. They only require good partnerships, a solid, private Generative AI infrastructure that doesn't leak intellectual property to third parties, and a solid understanding of prompt generation, existing tools, and creative ways to combine them. This section should give a sense of the many diverse areas where leaders can drive innovation and efficiency in their own business operations.

8.2.1 Marketing

1. Generate highly customized e-mails

2. Automate responses to customer queries

3. Deploy hyper-personalized website chat agents to incentivize buying activity

4. Dedicate LLM instances to high-paying customers for deep understanding of their context and history

5. Create customized copy based on demographics

6. Automate A/B copy generation and image generation

7. Develop social media graphics

8. Generate personalized product recommendations

9. Automate content generation for blogs and articles

10. Analyze customer data to identify trends and preferences

8.2.2 Software Engineering

11. Develop and generate code and unit tests

12. Automate code documentation

13. Automatically explain entire repositories of code to new employees

14. Generate prototype code

15. Port code from one language to another

16. Port code from one platform to another

17. Summarize requirements specification documents

18. Automate code refactoring

19. Generate code for API integration

8.2.3   Mechanical, Electrical, & Industrial Engineering

20. Generate CAD drawings from prompts

21. Generate documents that explain CAD packages

22. Generate circuit designs

23. Ideate physical tests for designs and equipment

24. Generate requirements for engineering projects

25. Compare product specifications and generate feature tables

26. Automate generation of bills of materials (BOMs)

27. Optimize product designs using Generative AI algorithms

28. Automate generation of manufacturing instructions

29. Generate simulations and analysis reports for product testing

8.2.4   Cybersecurity & Information Technology

30. Generate test plans

31. Analyze documentation and create asset lists

32. Generate command line instructions to conduct penetration and other types of tests

33. Analyze log files and identify anomalies

34. Convert log files into document summaries

35. Develop Kubernetes, Docker, and other DevOps deployment scripts and configuration files

36. Automate vulnerability assessments, malware analysis, and detection

37. Generate security incident reports

38. Assist in the detection and prevention of cyber threats

8.2.5   Sales

39. Generate and check custom e-mail copy and customer responses

40. Summarize company marketing documents into a paragraph for inclusion in responses

41. Analyze online company lists and determine if any fit target criteria

42. Develop custom e-mails based on the backgrounds of particular executives

43. Check message tone; ensure that emotion can be managed by the LLM at post-processing

44. Automate lead scoring and qualification

45. Generate personalized sales presentations

46. Analyze customer data to identify cross-selling and upselling opportunities

47. Automate sales forecasting and pipeline management

48. Automate customer relationship management (CRM) tasks

49. Analyze customer feedback and sentiment analysis for sales insights

50. Generate sales performance reports and dashboards

51. Automate contract generation and negotiation

52. Assist in pricing optimization and discounting strategies

53. Generate personalized product catalogs and recommendations for sales representatives

54. Automate customer onboarding processes

55. Assist in territory mapping and sales route optimization

56. Generate sales training materials and simulations

8.2.6 Finance and Accounting

57. Generate Excel formulas based on text prompts

58. Generate document outlines, such as investor relations updates

59. Automate aspects of due diligence by analyzing documents automatically

60. Analyze financial data to identify patterns and anomalies

61. Automate financial reporting and statement generation

62. Generate budgeting and forecasting models

63. Assist in risk assessment and compliance monitoring

64. Automate invoice processing and accounts payable and receivable tasks

65. Generate financial performance analysis reports

66. Assist in tax planning and optimization

8.2.7 Legal

67. Generate standard documents such as NDAs (Non-Disclosure Agreements)

68. Customize documents by asking for clauses in plain English and having an input document automatically modified

69. Summarize complex legal language into plain English

70. Automate contract review and analysis

71. Assist in legal research and case law analysis

72. Generate legal briefs, memos, contracts, and agreements

73. Automate document redaction for sensitive information

74. Assist in legal document discovery and e-discovery processes

75. Analyze contracts for potential risks and non-compliance

8.3   The Journey Ahead

As we stand on the brink of a future shaped by Generative AI, the path forward is marked by immense promise and some challenges. This technology has the potential to revolutionize our lives and work in ways we are only beginning to understand. At the same time, it poses complex questions about ethics, security, privacy, and social impact that we must grapple with.

We need to navigate this journey with care and foresight, acknowledging the complexity and dynamism of the landscape. It is not a path that we can traverse in a straight line, but one that requires us to adapt and pivot as we learn more about the technology and its implications.

The responsibility of steering this journey lies not with a single group but is shared among all stakeholders—technologists, policymakers, business leaders, and society at large.

Each group has a critical role to play, and their actions need to be guided by a shared commitment to ethical principles, societal benefit, and the sustainable use of technology.

8.4   A Call to Action

Generative AI isn't simply a technology or tool. It is the dawn of a new era, a paradigm shift, and a fresh approach to problem solving. It is the embodiment of human imagination and creativity, bolstered by computing power. Adopting this technology transcends the boundaries of being just competitive or innovative. It is about visualizing a future where tech takes on humanity's cause, bolstering our potential and spreading our collective wisdom.

To the leaders, CEOs, and visionaries, the call to action is clear. Engage in this transformative journey, partner for success, cultivate a fertile ground for innovation intertwined with ethical responsibility, and lead institutions into the age of AI. Unearth the profound potential of LLMs and Generative AI, grasp their capacity to reforge industries, comprehend their relevance to your business. Carve out strategies that harness these potent technologies effectively and ethically. Build a nurturing environment where employees and partners are emboldened to innovate with AI, and where AI ethics are the backbone of an organization's culture.

To the pioneers, researchers, and developers—continue to push the envelope. Generative AI feels different. It feels like we are almost arriving at that long-awaited place where machine intelligence will become increasingly indistinguishable from human intelligence. Aim high with transparency and efficiency in mind. And keep your feet grounded in ethics. You are the architects of a future that has dwelt in the realm of imagination for millennia.

To the policymakers and legislators, your role is of utmost

importance. Craft holistic, adaptable policies that shepherd AI use without impacting the productivity of business. As these technologies gain momentum, it is paramount we have robust, flexible regulations ensuring ethical and responsible use. We should curb the tendency to over-regulate and instead lean on regulations already in place, wherever possible, such as those on privacy, export controls, and others. We do require guidelines that foster innovation while safeguarding our citizens and upholding our values, but we should not create roadblocks to our companies moving fast and staying ahead.

Educators, it is time to usher AI into classrooms. As we journey deeper into the AI epoch, it is indispensable that our successors are fluent in AI. Equip our children not just with the skills to wield AI, but the discernment to evaluate it— how it really works and how it can be applied for their benefit, its boons, its risks, and its moral implications.

And to all readers, let's not forget—AI is a tool of our creation. It is a long-held human aspiration. Its purpose is to serve us, to aid us in overcoming challenges, and to enrich our existence. As we continue to shape our technological future, let us remember that at the heart of this development lies our desire to transcend the harder, darker parts of our human experience.

To the creators and consumers of technology, recognize the transformative power of AI in your hands. This revolution will be many times what the personal communications revolution was with cell phones in its ability to impact our daily lives, commerce, and the economy. As you use these new tools that augment your knowledge and understanding, focus on their immense capacity and potential to help you do more and do better. But do remember their limitations. Trust, but verify. Apply discernment. Use AI responsibly, considerately, and creatively, remembering that for now, it is a tool designed to enhance, not replace, human intelligence and intuition.

And finally, to our future generations, we are laying the groundwork for you to build upon. Without artificial intelligence, there can be no persistent presence in space. Without AI, there can be no believable Metaverse, no freeing of ourselves from the tyranny of dangerous labor. Embrace the challenges and opportunities presented by AI, wield it with wisdom and care, and continue to elevate the potential of our human race.

While often it seems daunting, we can indeed rise to the occasion collectively. The future is a shared narrative, and it is upon us to write a tale of progress, compassion, and ingenuity, underpinned by the transformative power of Generative AI. The dawn of the new era is here. Let's step into it with knowledge, courage, and a commitment to creating a world where technology is not the "other"—not the enemy— but our ally in creating a future that we can be proud of.

Bibliography

[1] *Meritalk, DOD Leaders: Don't Stop the Generative AI Research*, https://www.meritalk.com/articles/dod-leaders-dont-stop-the-generative-ai-research/

[2] Towards Data Science, *Your Car May Not Know When to Stop: Adversarial Attacks Against Autonomous Vehicles*, https://towardsdatascience.com/your-car-may-not-know-when-to-stop-adversarial-attacks-against-autonomous-vehicles-a16df91511f4

[3] KXAN, *UT Austin Researchers Tackle AI that Produced 'White Obama' Image*, https://www.kxan.com/news/local/austin/ut-austin-researchers-tackle-ai-that-produced-white-obama-image/

[4] Wikipedia, *Dennis Ritchie*, https://en.wikipedia.org/wiki/Dennis_Ritchie#/media/File:Ken_Thompson_and_ Dennis_Ritchie--1973.jpg

[5] Kevin Eykholt, Ivan Evtimov, Earlence Fernandes, Bo Li, Amir Rahmati, Chaowei Xiao, Atul Prakash, Tadayoshi Kohno, Dawn Song, *Robust Physical-World Attacks on Deep Learning Visual Classification*, University of Michigan, Ann Arbor, University of Washington, University of California, Berkeley, Samsung Research America and Stony Brook University, https://arxiv.org/pdf/1707.08945.pdf

[6] sUAS News, *Daedalean Concluded a Joint Research*

BIBLIOGRAPHY

Project with the FAA on Neural Network-Based Runway Landing Guidance for General Aviation, 2022, https://www.suasnews.com/2022/05/daedalean-concluded-a-joint-research-project-with-the-faa-on-neural-network-based-runway-landing-guidance-for-general-aviation/

[7] Yahoo Finance, *SparkCognition and Shell Announce Technology Collaboration*, 2023, https://finance.yahoo.com/news/sparkcognition-shell-announce-technology-collaboration-115500355.html

[8] ITP.net, *AI is the beating heart of Saudi Arabia's NEOM*, says CEO, 2023, https://www.itp.net/emergent-tech/ai-is-the-beating-heart-of-saudi-arabias-neom-says-ceo

[9] Amir Husain, *AH Generative Designer*, https://openworks. cc/gd/

[10] *OpenAI's attempts to watermark AI text hit limits*, TechCrunch, https://techcrunch.com/2022/12/10/openais-attempts-to-watermark-ai-text-hit-limits/

[11] *The Literacy Project*, https://literacyproj.org/

[12] *Sam Altman of OpenAI testifies before Congress*, CNN, https://www.cnn.com/2023/05/16/tech/sam-altman-openai-congress/index.html

[13] *Artificial Intelligence Act*, European Union, https://artificialintelligenceact.eu/

[14] *Schumer courts bipartisan lawmakers on AI regulation*, Fox News, https://www.foxnews.com/politics/

chuck-schumer-courts-bipartisan-lawmakers-ai-regulation

[15] *Fact Sheet: Biden-Harris Administration Announces New Actions to Promote Responsible AI Innovation That Protects Americans' Rights and Safety*, The White House, https://www.whitehouse.gov/briefing-room/statements-re-leases/2023/05/04/fact-sheet-biden-harris-administra-tion-announces-new-actions-to-promote-responsible-ai-in-novation-that-protects-americans-rights-and-safety/

[16] *How quickly are China's ChatGPT-style services catching up with Microsoft-backed OpenAI?*, South China Morn-ing Post, https://www.scmp.com/tech/tech-trends/ar-ticle/3220062/how-quickly-are-chinas-ChatGPT-style-services-catching-microsoft-backed-openai

[17] *Volkswagen Applies Generative Design*, Automation World, https://www.automationworld.com/products/software/blog/13320039/volkswagen-applies-genera-tive-design

[18] *Generative Design*, Wikipedia, https://en.wikipedia.org/ wiki/Generative_design

[19] *Fishing Pliers Reimagined With Generative Design*, All-3DP, https://all3dp.com/4/fishing-pliers-reimag-ined-with-generative-design/

[20] Matt Pearson, *Generative Art: A practical guide using Processing.* Manning Publications, https://www.man-ning.com/books/generative-art.

[21] Joseph Babcock and Raghav Bali. Generative AI with

Python and TensorFlow 2: Create images, text, and music with VAEs, GANs, LSTMs, Transformer models. Packt Publishing.

[22] Amir Husain. *The Sentient Machine: The Coming Age of Artificial Intelligence*. Scribner.

[23] Amir Husain, John R. Allen, Robert O. Work. *Hyperwar: Conflict and Competition in the AI Century*. SparkCognition Press.

[24] Amir Husain. *Twitter Thread by Amir Husain on the UNIX Philosophy*. Twitter. https://twitter.com/amirhusain_tx/ status/1435082110121955330

[25] Jacob Devlin, Ming-Wei Chang, Kenton Lee, Kristina Toutanova, BERT: Pre-training of Deep Bidirectional Transformers for Language Understanding, arXiv:1810.04805 [cs.CL] (2019)

[26] Vidur Joshi, Matthew Peters, Mark Hopkins, *Extending a Parser to Distant Domains Using a Few Dozen Partially Annotated Examples*, arXiv:1805.06556 [cs.CL] (2018)

[27] Mansi Rawat, *An Introduction to Saliency Maps in Deep Learning*, Reddit, March 7, 2022, https://www.marktechpost.com/2022/03/07/an-introduction-to-saliency-maps-in-deep-learning/

[28] Sujit Rokka Chhetri, A. Lopez, and M. A. Faruque, *GAN-Sec: Generative Adversarial Network Modeling for the Security Analysis of Cyber-Physical Production Systems*, Published 1 March 2019, Computer Science, In Pro-

ceedings of the 2019 Design, Automation & Test in Europe Conference & Exhibition.

[29] Marqual IT Solutions Pvt. Ltd (KBV Research), *North America Generative AI Market Size, Share & Industry Trends Analysis Report,* Country and Growth Forecast, 2022 - 2028, December 2022, On Research and Markets.

[30] Hanneke Weitering, *How Artificial Intelligence Could Completely Reshape Aircraft Future, FutureFlight.* https://www.futureflight.aero/news-article/2023-05-20/how-artificial-intelligence-could-completely-reshape-aircraft-future

Index

A

B

C

D

P

Palantir 67
Porter, Bruce 10
printing, 3D 27, 28, 29
ProWritingAid 101
Python 66, 68
PyTorch 66

Q

QuillBot 101

R

Recurrent Neural Network (RNN) 87, 104
Requena, Guto 78

S

SageMaker 66
Samba 78
Schaefer, Bastien 27
Schumer, Chuck 120
security 8, 11, 13, 14, 41, 42, 45, 53, 55, 57, 65, 66, 70, 75, 83, 94, 114, 125, 127, 130, 133
sequence prediction 4, 5, 12, 25, 41, 84, 87, 88, 104, 106
Shell 9, 10, 11, 117
Skinner, Robert 44
SparkCognition 9, 10, 11, 58, 59, 67, 79, 117
Stony Brook University 80
Sustainable Aerospace Together Forum 83

T

TensorFlow 65, 66
Theano 66
Time Machine conference 79
transfer learning 91, 96
Transformer 2, 6, 61, 66, 88, 97
Transformer-based model 2, 12, 14, 61, 87, 97, 104

U

University of California at Berkeley 42

INDEX

About the Author

Amir Husain is the Founder & CEO of AI unicorn, Spark-Cognition, the Founding CEO of SkyGrid, a Boeing, Spark-Cognition company, and the Chairman of Navigate, a Web3 business building a crowd-sourced data marketplace. He has been named Austin's Top Technology Entrepreneur of the Year and received the Austin Under 40 Technology and Science Award, along with several other accolades recognizing his work in artificial intelligence.

Amir serves on the Board of Advisors for The University of Texas at Austin Department of Computer Science and on the NATO Maritime Unmanned Systems Innovation Advisory Board. He is also a member of the Council on Foreign Relations.

In 2020, Amir joined the inaugural Board of Spark-Cognition Government Systems (SGS), the world's first full-spectrum AI company devoted entirely to government and national defense, chaired by former Deputy Secretary of Defense, Robert O. Work.

Amir has been awarded over 30 patents and has several pending applications. His work has been featured in world-leading outlets such as Foreign Policy, Fox Business News, Forbes, and Proceedings from the U.S. Naval Institute. He is the author of the best-selling book *The Sentient Machine: The Coming Age of Artificial Intelligence* and a co-author of the compilation *Hyperwar: Conflict and Competition in the AI Century.*